# The "Disciple Investing" Life

# The "Disciple Investing" Life

Helping Others Grow in Their Relationship with Christ

ROD CULBERTSON

WIPF & STOCK · Eugene, Oregon

Wipf & Stock
An Imprint of Wipf and Stock Publishers
199 W. 8th Ave., Suite 3
Eugene, OR 97401

www.wipfandstock.com

PAPERBACK ISBN: 978-1-5326-0694-6
HARDCOVER ISBN: 978-1-5326-0696-0
EBOOK ISBN: 978-1-5326-0695-3

Manufactured in the U.S.A.                                      01/16/17

With the deepest gratitude to my Lord and Savior, Jesus Christ, who called me to himself in 1972 and continues to patiently disciple me throughout this life, I dedicate this book to the glory of the triune God: Father, Son, and Holy Spirit. May our almighty God use this work in order that his kingdom shall come and his will be done on earth, as it is in heaven.

In addition to the gift of eternal life, Christ bestowed upon me a most dedicated life helper in my beloved wife, Catherine Wooten Culbertson, who has never hesitated to follow him and to sacrifice herself for my benefit and well-being, as well as for our children and his church. I am eternally grateful to him for her love and faithfulness, and remain one who is blessed beyond measure!

# Contents

# Acknowledgements

First and foremost, I want to thank the triune God, who, in his great love, chose me to be his own from all eternity, a total act of grace. All glory be to the one who called me to the privilege and joy of being a disciple of Jesus Christ, our Lord. He called and I have never regretted following.

I thank him for giving me a mother, the late Virginia Sample Culbertson, who would raise me in the fear and admonition of the Lord, and point me toward the cross of Christ for my salvation.

I cannot list all of the people who have influenced me in my walk as a disciple of Christ, but I thank God for sending some very special people into my life who have caused me to look to Jesus for all of life: Rev. Mr. "J" Thompson, Mack Graham Jr., Dr. Ken Compton, Charles C. "Buddy" Smith, Dr. John O. Bumgardner, Rev. Mr. Al Lutz, the late Rev. Mr. Buck Hatch, the late Dr. William Larkin, Rev. Mr. Laurie Vidal, Rev. Mr. Mark Lowrey, the late Pierre and Betty Vidal, Larry Eubanks, Rev. Mr. G. Dale Linder, Henry and Carol Vierling, Roy Heintz, Dr. Ric Cannada, and the late Francis Schaeffer, who through his writings made a profound and lasting impact on my need to be a loving follower of Christ.

A special word of thanks must be given to my two RTS Charlotte teaching assistants, Mrs. Anna Page Portillo, and Ms. Anna Unkefer, who spent countless hours editing this work and refining it for publication. And finally, I must thank two other readers of the work, who most certainly helped to improve it, Mrs. Tari Williamson, Dean of Women at RTS Charlotte, and RTS student, Mrs. Karen Chacko. All of these ladies' assistance was invaluable.

# Introduction

## My Story

I WAS A FEW weeks into my freshman year at the University of South Carolina walking down the sidewalk between the reflection pond and the Thomas Cooper Library. I was on my way back to my dorm room, having just finished up a Sunday lunch at the Russell House Student Union cafeteria. I was hustling to my dorm, trying to figure out how to use the remainder of my afternoon. And there they stood. Three guys in conversation, and from the looks of it, easily one student standing with a couple of religious recruiter types. Two of the guys, apparently students, were persuading a third student to hear them out; I had seen similar fundamentalist style encounters on Main Street while growing up in my hometown of Greenville, South Carolina, and it made me quite nervous. Although God had been dealing with me–a typical prodigal freshman student–I had no interest whatsoever in being a target of these religious do-gooders. I would avoid them at all costs.

However, God had other plans. Just as I veered off south of the sidewalk the third student had his fill of the discussion and left. The two recruiters simultaneously turned and saw me standing there just a few feet away: foiled! Their first words, which I still remember clearly, were, "Excuse me, but we are starting a Bible study on campus and wondered if you might be interested?" Of course, even though I had been attending church on Sunday mornings, was sensing that I might fail out of my first semester in college, and though it appeared that God was working me over pretty well, I had no interest whatsoever. The short story is that I tried everything I could to deflect their pressure (which really wasn't that strong). But eventually I took their information and departed with it in hand. The new Bible study would start the next night at 7:00 pm at the USC International House on the other side of campus from my dorm. I would *not* be there!

As I continued down the sidewalk toward the Longstreet Theater and Sumter Street (confident that I had dodged a bullet), it was as if I were walking with my back toward God–and I was. However, before I reached the steps to Green Street, I sensed that the Lord was speaking to me, not audibly, but simply and firmly to my heart. As odd as it may seem, I looked back and up, feeling as if I was indeed running from God; he certainly seemed far away because I had turned my back on him. But I heard him say to my heart, "What do I have to do in order to get your attention?" That was enough! I considered my recent circumstances, and on the spot, I made a commitment to the Lord, "I will be at that Bible study tomorrow night." Honestly, I had made many similar religious promises and commitments to God in the past, but I knew I must keep this one.

Monday evening came, classes were finished, dinner was done, and I knew it was time to go-yes, to attend the Bible study. With a sense of both dread and resignation, I pulled out my childhood, black, King James Version of the Bible, well-hidden in the back of my desk drawer so that no one else could know that I actually had taken a Bible with me to college. Hiding it under my arm as best as I could, and filled with embarrassment that I might be "found out," that evening I took the long trek across campus to the International Student House. When I finally arrived, I met the few guys (maybe six) who had shown up for this inaugural Bible study. There were some awkward moments of introduction and the Bible study began. Without including all of the details, I must say that not only was God working, he was working powerfully in me. For the first time in my life, though having been raised in the church from infancy, and having attended almost everything the church offered, I found myself interested in what God had to say. Of course, I had been interested a good deal in the past, but not enough to want to give him my life, or my all. However, either on that reflection pool sidewalk, or in my dorm room, or on the way to the Bible study, or possibly during the Bible study, I had been converted, i.e., made new and alive (the scholars call it "regenerated"; the revivalists call it "born again"). I was now a true disciple of Jesus Christ; it was all so very new and there was no turning back for me!

The Bible study I attended that night was the first ever meeting on the USC campus of a Christian organization known as "The Navigators"! Distinguished by their emphasis on discipleship, the Navigators were a ministry that, in addition to First Baptist Church of Columbia, guided me in finding and knowing Jesus Christ. In the coming years, I would discover that through the impact and influence of all types of ministries, individuals and other sources, I was ultimately being (and am still being) discipled by Jesus Christ, the risen, living Savior. He graciously and sovereignly called me to himself that Sunday afternoon, and that call was a simple and profound "Follow Me!" I knew that if I were going to truly follow Jesus as his disciple, it would mean giving up myself and making him first in everything. He would take me by the hand, so to speak, and guide me along the way.

This is the manner of discipleship: Jesus, walking alongside us, his followers, working his will in our lives, and guiding and teaching us through the power of the Holy Spirit who indwells believers. The Holy Spirit is in charge of the entire process because the Holy Spirit is truly the One who orchestrates the discipleship process.

## The Great Commandment and The Great Commission

Ultimately, as we are discipled by Jesus and, in turn, help others to grow in their walks with Christ, we are privileged to be a part of the joyful obedience that is found in responding to both Jesus's Great Commandment and Jesus's Great Commission. In Matthew 22, we read the following words,

> 37 Jesus replied: "'Love the Lord your God with all your heart and with all your soul and with all your mind.' 38 This is the first and greatest commandment. 39 And the second is like it: 'Love your neighbor as yourself.' 40 All the Law and the Prophets hang on these two commandments."

What a blessed possibility we have to be conduits of the love of God to other people. As we learn to love the living God who made us and redeemed us, we are able more and more to find a fountain of love that overflows in our hearts and out of our lives to the people around us. Disciple investing is just that: loving others with the love that God has demonstrated toward us, in that, while we were still sinners, Christ died for us![1] The primary desire and focus of every believer must be to learn to love God first and foremost. We give him our hearts and our lives with a passion and emotion that expresses gratitude for our salvation. If we are passionate for the living God, and our love for him is growing and steady, we will not only be responding properly to the First and Greatest Commandment, but we will

---

1. Rom 5:8.

also find the desire and ability to seek to fulfill the Second Commandment. Of course, we recognize that we cannot come close to loving God with all of our hearts, souls, and minds–we fail miserably. But in our hearts, we know whether or not there is at least a fire burning for God, even if what we and others see is mostly smoke. Our inability to love God fully is the impetus that drives us to the cross and causes us to rely upon the Holy Spirit who indeed has poured out the love of Christ in our hearts.[2] Here is where the motivation for disciple investing–helping others know Jesus–begins: loving God wholeheartedly. If you love God, you will be enabled to love people through the power of his love working through you.

I believe that living out the Great Commandment is absolutely essential to obeying the Great Commission that Jesus gave his disciples prior to departing bodily from this earth. One of the most familiar passages in the Bible, even for the newest Christian, is Jesus's declaration to his disciples known as *The Great Commission*. These powerful, commanding, and authoritative words, as recorded at the end of the gospel of Matthew, occur after his resurrection and before his ascension into heaven,

> 16 Now the eleven disciples went to Galilee, to the mountain to which Jesus had directed them. 17 And when they saw him they worshiped him, but some doubted. 18 And Jesus came and said to them, "All authority in heaven and on earth has been given to me. 19 Go therefore and make disciples of all nations, baptizing them in the name of the Father and of the Son and of the Holy Spirit, 20 teaching them to observe all that I have commanded you. And behold, I am with you always, to the end of the age."

In these brief sentences, Jesus proclaims the mission of the church to his astounded followers. The previously disheveled twelve (minus Judas) wonder when the kingdom of God will occur. Instead of remaining and reigning, Jesus explains that he is departing and declaring, handing his disciples a monumental task: that of reaching the entire world with his message of atonement (his finished work on the cross): forgiveness and repentance unto eternal life.

The resurrection of their Lord and Savior is the only reality that might spawn such zeal as was demonstrated by the disciples in the ensuing days. Love for God and for their neighbor could be the only genuine motivation for heeding Christ's commission. Of course, they would need the falling and coming of the Holy Spirit at Pentecost, as promised by Jesus, to provide the

2. Rom 5:5.

power and the impetus for the message of the gospel to go forth with great effect. Sacrificial love, as demonstrated by their Savior and Lord, would be a necessary ingredient in gospel motivation and proclamation. Love God and love your neighbor? What could be a better way than to tell and teach others, i.e., everyone, the nations, everything that the resurrected Lord of life had commanded them? Bring them to Jesus, teach them about Jesus, and baptize them into the local church in the name of the three persons of the Trinity: Father, Son, and Holy Spirit. Can you do it? Can you love God and others? Jesus promises that he will be present with his disciples always, even to the end. I believe that his presence with and in us will help us love others into his wonderful kingdom of light. And there, in his kingdom, we can be a part of the process of investing in Jesus's followers, while watching them grow. Consider the possibility. Are you ready and willing?

## Disciple Investing is for You!

Over the many years of my life, college students, campus ministry staff, pastors, friends, Sunday School teachers, peers, Scripture reading (as well as memorization and meditation), prayer meetings, evangelism training and opportunities, church deacons and elders, baseball and basketball coaches, university and seminary professors, conference and seminar speakers, pamphlets and books, radio and television ministers, various film and video series, Christian musicians, choral events, Christian service opportunities, and a host of other influences have discipled me. Yet, it is my contention (and the basic premise of this book) that Jesus primarily loves to use ordinary people–believers–as the conduits of his ministry in others' lives. Jesus, the supreme discipler, is doing the work and we are simply investing in others as a part of his plan. We are cooperating with Jesus as his faithful, humble servants. As his followers, having been made alive by the Spirit, we naturally want to be a part of the building and extension of Christ's Kingdom. You, or any believer, can contribute to the nurture and growth of another believer (or even the conversion of an unbeliever) if you are willing to try. Jesus can use *you*! You can be a part of Jesus's process of discipling others simply by investing yourself in their lives. How exciting! And that is what this short book is about.

After I became a Christian, many people spoke into my life and gave me guidance. Some gave me counsel and supported me in my struggles as a young man and a new believer (and those struggles were often seemingly overwhelming, and at times both fearful and tearful). Others led by example or even from a distance. But their influence did not go unnoticed. The list of names of people who helped me as a new believer is too long to acknowledge here. Some would not even remember me; yet I remember them with fondness and gratitude. Jesus used them to help me grow, love God more, follow him and become more like him. And ever since I came to Christ, I have similarly watched Jesus use me in the lives of others as well. Most of these stories are under the radar and are certainly not what some would call glamorous success stories. I haven't amassed any fame or notoriety in my ministries or through my personal involvement in the lives of others. At this stage of my life, it is doubtful that I ever will. I haven't made any headlines and don't expect to do so. However, it doesn't matter, for I believe that most ministry (pastoral or layperson) is simply carried out in the day-to-day living and sharing of ordinary life with others who are a God-ordained part of our world.

With that perspective in mind, I must also state that initiative and willingness to be involved in the lives of others is absolutely essential to what I call the "disciple investing" life. When I look back at my ministry, from college student, continuing in seminary, on to campus ministry and later in church planting, as well as in working with seminary students at Reformed Theological Seminary, the deepest and most rewarding relationships for me have occurred with those in whom I have personally invested the most heavily. Almost without exception, the more personally I was involved in another's life or others' lives, the more blessed I was to be a part of what Jesus was doing in them and to see *him* actually working through me, an inadequate sinner. This was an amazing truth: I discovered that he could and would use me, as I was willing to be used by him to help others grow or learn. The bottom line to "successful" disciple investing is simply to have interest in the spiritual well-being of another individual or a group of individuals, and to give yourself willingly to them. Anyone, even the most extreme introvert, can do this through the power of the indwelling Holy Spirit. The life and enablement is his to give–and *you* can do it.

## What is Disciple Investing?

Discipleship is following Jesus. Discipleship is becoming a person who learns from Jesus. Discipleship is learning to love Jesus, the living Lord and Savior. Discipleship is a process which involves a full-orbed, multi-dimensional impact by the Holy Spirit in the life of the follower of Jesus Christ. Simply put, discipleship is the process by which God changes us to be more and more like his son.

My personal definition (a lengthy one) of a disciple of Jesus is this:

> A Christian disciple is one who, by God's grace, has become a learner, a lover, and a follower of Jesus Christ. This follower is one who walks by faith in relationship with the risen Christ, and whose mind, emotions, and will are submitted to and changed by Christ's Word and his Spirit, so that the disciple obediently loves the triune God more and more, is becoming conformed to Christ's likeness more and more, and serves more and more in his body, the church. The process of discipleship occurs in the community of Christ's church and involves multiple and various avenues of influence—people, home life, activities, personal experiences, ministries outside of the church—in such a way that Jesus Christ uses "all of life" to sovereignly work in *his* disciple's life in order to glorify the heavenly Father. When a person becomes engaged in this process with another individual, he/she is simply investing in the discipling work that Jesus himself is doing in that individual's life.

The above definition attempts to demonstrate that disciple building is something that Jesus is doing, as his followers invest in others to help them follow him fully. I wish to emphasize that the whole person is impacted by the gospel and that this change of life is initiated by God's grace. Discipleship begins as one hears the gospel message and believes in God's Word; then God works in the individual's heart. The disciple is a responder to God's initiative and responds in a comprehensive fashion with a willingness to follow, obey, and submit himself to the Lord. This person becomes a learner (the mind), a lover (the emotions and heart), and a follower (the will). All three domains (mind, heart, and will) of the disciple's being are transformed.

The disciple walks by faith, believing and trusting God, the loving Father, to accomplish his purposes through her. She experiences the presence and fellowship of Jesus and by faith walks hand-in-hand with him. The follower is wholly devoted and reliant upon both the active Word of God and the leading, guiding, and empowering presence of the indwelling Holy Spirit. Using the means of grace with full reliance upon the work of the Holy Spirit is absolutely necessary for any follower of Christ to grow. One can see that the Trinity is involved in the life of the disciple, and nothing can be more reassuring for the believer than that reality. Consequently, the true fruit of discipleship is service to the body of Christ, more specifically: to Christ's body as expressed in the local church. The ultimate goal of disciple investing is a life lived wholeheartedly for the glory of the triune God!

## Self Assessment

Let me ask you just a few questions about your own present or past involvement in Christian growth and discipleship, and maybe you will be intrigued by this critical subject:

- Have you ever spent time meeting with a more mature Christian in a one-to-one fashion, and on a regular basis in order to learn more about Christ, the Bible, or the Christian life?

- If another person did invest in your life, was it a pastor, campus staff or minister, a layperson in the church, a peer, or someone else? Why did this person initiate your meeting(s)?

- If another person did invest in your life, what does this past investment in you mean to you personally today? How did this person impact you?

- Similarly, have you personally ever spent time meeting with a new believer or less mature Christian in a one-to-one fashion in order to help him/her learn more about Christ, the Bible, or the Christian life?

- Have you ever asked someone if you could meet with him *just once* to discuss how to live the Christian life?

- Have you ever asked someone if you could meet with her *on a regular basis* to discuss how to live the Christian life, or what a Christian should believe about God and the Bible?

- Have you ever sought out someone for guidance or counsel regarding the Christian life, or problems with which you were struggling?

- Have you ever met with another Christian on a regular basis for mutual help, listening, discussion, or as a sounding board?

- Has anyone ever helped you understand how to have a daily devotional life that includes prayer, Bible reading, and Christian meditation? Have you ever helped another person with the same task?

- Have you ever been trained or taught how to be a witness for Christ, or how to explain the gospel? Can you explain the basics of the gospel? Could you train someone else in how to explain the gospel?

As you think about your answers to these various questions, I would like to pose my basic premise to you once more: disciple investing is something you can be involved in and also something that you can do. God can use your efforts, energy, time, and attention to help change another person's life. Of course, it is Christ who is using you and Christ, through his Spirit and Word, who is doing the transformation. But you have the potential to make a difference. We will discuss the possibilities of what you can do and how to do it in the coming chapters.

## Questions for Reflection

1. According to this chapter, how are the Great Commandment and the Great Commission related to each other?

2. Which aspect of being a disciple is the most natural for you: 1) learning–reading, studying, and thinking; 2) loving–caring for others and the expressing of emotions; 3) following (doing)–being involved in ministry and activity on behalf of the Lord, the church, and others? How can you improve upon your weaknesses?

3. What are some of the avenues that have helped you grow as a Christian? What are the differences (advantages/disadvantages) between personal involvement (other people affecting your life) and "impersonal" involvement (books, blogs, television programs, etc.) in the disciple investing process?

4. What are some of the possible benefits of investing in another person's spiritual walk with Christ?

## Action Points

1. Make a list of 3–5 people who have invested themselves in your walk with Christ.

2. Write a letter or note to someone who has impacted your life for Christ, thanking them and letting them know how you are doing today.

# 1

# Qualifications (Qualities That Count)

IF I HAVE CONVINCED you thus far that you can not only be a disciple of Christ (which you are, if you know him personally), but that you can actually assist another believer (or believers) in his/her Christian growth, then we need to talk about a few basic requirements or qualifications necessary for the task. What are the attributes of a person who wishes to invest in another's Christian growth and progress? The reality is that the qualities that are fundamental to helping others grow in their walks with Jesus are the same qualities that the early disciples demonstrated while they followed Jesus during his pilgrimage here on earth.

## A Walk with Christ

The first qualification–and one that might appear obvious–is that the disciple investor must be a person who is walking with Jesus daily through life. That is to say, the disciple investor must know Christ personally, not simply by mere profession of faith, but in an active and vibrant relationship in which Christ is very real and present to the follower. Is this you? Are you looking to Jesus each day in order to listen to him, respond to, and follow him with your whole heart? Granted, there are always failures and lapses in our efforts to walk with Christ, and sin can enter in as well, but are you moving forward? Are you repenting of your nagging, persistent sins? Are you looking to Jesus for his help and presence, and do you sense his nearness even when you sometimes feel far from him? Is Jesus both your Lord and friend in your personal walk through life? What does this mean? Some decades ago in 1971, when I was a teenager, a musical known as *Godspell* hit Broadway. (I admit, I never saw it–I heard that Jesus was portrayed as a clown.) Overnight it became a sensation, possibly promoted by the catchy theme song written by Stephen Schwartz and sung by someone by the name of Robin Lamont. The song hit the billboards in 1973 and became a popular public chorus, sung and hummed by many in the West (America and Europe) who heard it. The song was entitled "Day by Day" and known for its simple and easily memorized lyrics:

> Day by day, day by day, oh, dear Lord, three things I pray
> To see thee more clearly
> Love thee more dearly
> Follow thee more nearly, day by day
>
> Day by day, day by day
> Oh, dear Lord, three things I pray. . .

Interestingly, the story behind this song is that the captivating chorus drew its three line refrain from a prayer ascribed to the thirteenth-century English bishop Saint Richard of Chichester (possibly on his deathbed). Although history is unclear whether Bishop Richard actually composed the rhyming refrain (the words were translated from Latin into English and probably embellished by the translator), the *Godspell* rendition certainly provided a basic description of a vital walk with God. "To see the Lord more clearly" addresses the need of the believer to hear, read, study, and meditate upon God's holy Word, the Bible, as the source in which he reveals himself. "To see" in this sense clearly focuses on the intellectual or *knowledge* domain of the heart. "To love thee more dearly" describes a deep desire to know the Lord intimately, with personal emotion and passion for his being, and focuses on the *affective* domain of the heart. Lastly, "To follow thee more nearly" ascribes a willingness (flowing from a heart of love) to obey and submit to the revealed will of God–a focus on the *volitional* domain of the heart. So my question to you, as a potential disciple investor is, "Are you walking with God?" Are you seeking him through his inspired Word, the Bible? Do you have a loving attachment to and desire for the personal God who made you? Are you seeking, wholeheartedly–despite your failures–to follow and obey him as you grow in understanding his revealed will? If so, he not only can use you but I believe he *will* use you as you seek to minister to others.

## A Flowing Fountain

Part of this growing walk with God involves learning to depend upon and trust in the Lord to provide the "life" of your daily journey. Christ is the source of all that you do for him. In John 15, Jesus says the following,

> 5 I am the vine; you are the branches. If you remain in me and I in you, you will bear much fruit; apart from me you can do nothing. 6 If you do not remain in me, you are like a branch that is thrown away and withers; such branches are picked up, thrown into the fire and burned. 7 If you remain in me and my words remain in you, ask whatever you wish, and it will be done for you. 8 This is to my Father's glory, that you bear much fruit, showing yourselves to be my disciples.

The person whom God uses to do the ministry of disciple investing grasps the great reality that it is the power of the indwelling God, through the Holy Spirit, who brings success or results to any venture on his behalf. Gaining one's life from the vine means always looking to him for strength, sustenance, and provision. We can do nothing without him, and yet with him, we can change the world one person at a time. But *we're* not changing anyone—*he* is doing it through us, as we depend on him. And he gets the glory that is due only to his name. The late, great nineteenth-century evangelist of Chicago, D.L. Moody, once said, "The only way to keep a broken vessel full is to keep the fountain flowing." I love that quote! It is liberating. We admittedly come to the Lord as broken vessels, broken by our sins, failures, inadequacies, deficiencies, and inabilities. But the branch is attached to the Vine! There is life. The broken vessel, filled with cracks small and large, can still hold water—at least some or enough to be useful—as long as the fountain (or the spigot, as is often used in our modern context) is pouring out water. The vine provides life to the often dangling branch. The fountain provides the life-giving sustenance of water to the broken vessel. And the spirit of Jesus uses the finite, failing believer, who trusts in him to do his work through him. Is the fountain flowing in your broken life?

## Faith that God will Work

If you are walking each day with God and learning to depend upon him for the fruit that he produces, it would seem logical to expect God to use you. Again, in John 15:5, Jesus says, "If you remain in me and I in you, you will bear much fruit. . ." He subsequently says in verses 7–8, "If you remain in me and my words remain in you, ask whatever you wish, and it will be done for you. This is to my Father's glory, that you bear much fruit, showing yourselves to be my disciples." God promises to use you! You can bear fruit in Jesus's kingdom! One aspect of the life of faith for the Christian is to trust God to work through your life, your words, your speaking, your teaching, your counsel, your comforting of others, and even through your silent presence in times of need, trial, or even joy and blessing. You serve the Lord, even taking risks or stepping out of your comfort zone, trusting that he will act. I was a campus minister at the University of Florida, serving with a ministry known as Reformed University Ministry (RUF today). While I was there, the RUF founder, the Reverend Mr. Mark Lowrey, would constantly remind us campus ministers of this one truth: God is at work! Many of the campus ministers in those early days of RUF worked on difficult campuses or had struggling ministries. Mark knew that every six months or so, when we had staff training (and there were usually less than ten of us), we needed encouragement to keep plugging away at our ministries, and to do so *by faith*. "God is at work!" In John 5:17, we read, "But Jesus answered them, 'My Father is working until now, and I am working.'" God the Father and God the Son are always working in this world. You can count on it! And the foundation of faith lies in both prayer and Scripture, to provide stronger faith for the seeking believer. So, labor, befriend, invest, contribute, listen, and counsel others who need you, and do so by faith. God will show up because he is always working and will bring himself glory by blessing your persistent efforts on his behalf!

## Fighting Sin

The normal Christian life is typified by spiritual warfare. In Ephesians 6, Paul writes about the need for the believer to put on the whole armor of God–wearing a "spiritual suit" necessary for spiritual battle against the schemes of the devil, and to enable her to withstand the evil day. Paul also writes in Galatians 5,

> 16But I say, walk by the Spirit, and you will not gratify the desires of the flesh. 17For the desires of the flesh are against the Spirit, and the desires of the Spirit are against the flesh, for these are opposed to each other, to keep you from doing the things you want to do.

We are in a daily battle with the flesh. Do you feel the struggle? Are you winning? Sometimes, we don't sense that we are winning or that we have made much progress. But, Paul promises that as we rely on the Holy Spirit for help and power, we can win in this spiritual battle! Walking by the power of the Holy Spirit will keep you from "gratifying the desires of the flesh" and prevent you from "doing the things you [your fleshly self] want to do." Suffice it to say that if you have given up in this personal battle against sin and your self-centered fleshly desires, you will not be much help to anyone else. You must fight the battle. As a Christian soldier, go arm in arm with your fellow believer(s) into the battle. Disciple investing means messing with Satan and sin, getting dirty, and sometimes experiencing wounds. But, with God's help, the victory is ours! What joy occurs when we see the gradual progress that relying on God brings, especially when we have been a part of helping another believer conquer in the battle! Rise each morning prepared to engage in spiritual warfare and recognize that you are serving a great King in his kingdom.

# Friendship

With only one exception (and he wasn't an enemy), I don't believe that I have ever personally invested in the life of another person whom I did not consider to be a friend. At the least, I could say, "I like this person and am drawn to him. I could enjoy this relationship." (That one time took me well out of my comfort zone for a person who had some deep needs at the time.) Friendship provides an easy segue or bridge toward your personal willingness to help or assist another person in his walk with the Lord. Generally speaking, the closest relationships that I have developed over the years are the relationships that have lasted over the years, due to personally investing in another person, individually or in a group. Social media has allowed me to find some of my long lost friends from my earlier days of Christian life and ministry. What a blessing! These were, and still are, friends in Christ. We love to share our lives together in our "latter" years. You do not have to be a relational expert or a "people person" to be a friend. As a matter of fact, many of the personality inventories indicate that the introverted or quieter person is often more deeply loyal and seriously committed to a relationship than some of the more "fun loving"-type personalities. Anyone can be a friend, or at the least, function as a friend–by showing up and caring during the rough times and the successes of life. Disciple investing ultimately could be considered simply as Christian friendship or building friendships for a lifetime! That perspective would be appealing for anyone. Go for it!

## Consistency

I am a bit cautious in mentioning this characteristic as a qualification. Even as a seminary professor, I tell my students that, at times, I am not always consistent in my teaching or behavior. I'm not sure, of course, that anyone is completely consistent in an absolute sense. However, I wish to briefly address the fact that the disciple investor needs to both avoid living in such a way that others could accuse him of personal hypocrisy, and also to strive to follow through when making promises or plans. Predictability and accountability are very helpful qualities that build trust, while attempting to gain a hearing for ministry. Jesus, of course, addressed hypocrisy numerous times in his confrontations with the Pharisees. One prominent instance is seen in Matthew 15 where he says,

> 7 You hypocrites! Well did Isaiah prophesy of you, when he said:
> 8 "This people honors me with their lips, but their heart is far from me; 9 in vain do they worship me, teaching as doctrines the commandments of men."

By definition, hypocrisy is pretense: pretending to be something or someone that you are not. It is "putting on the mask." It is having a heart that is far from reality. It is a sure form of dishonesty. Disciple investing will never occur if there is hypocrisy in your life. Others will find you out! No intimate relationship or friendship can survive the context of hypocrisy. However, successful disciple investing can occur if you are honest about your inconsistencies. We all are inconsistent. Nevertheless, what I am appealing for is a genuineness that is so real and such a part of who you are that you will do all you can to live up to your word. Your actions toward, and interest in the other person must be sincere, and ultimately, dependable. You truly care for her and are a reliable partner with her as you seek to know the Lord better, together. Consistency means that the other person can count on you. You are conscientious and when you fail, you are honestly conscientious about that as well. Like the old-school doctors and pastors of a by-gone era, in this relationship, you are "on call." You are available to help, talk, listen, relate, and invest. Consistency means that the other person can count on you. To whom will she go when she needs spiritual advice or help? You–you've always been there! That is the fruit of consistency in a relationship.

## A Biblical Foundation

Simply stated, if you wish to help another person grow in his spiritual walk with Christ, you must recognize the need for the Word of God in your own life, and use it as a resource on a daily (or regular) basis. The Scriptures are the foundation for living the Christian life. Everywhere we turn in the Bible, from Abraham, Moses, Joshua, David, Ezra, Nehemiah, Peter and Paul (and the list goes on–not to mention Jesus), we see God's followers relying upon God's words and God's promises as a resource for faith and service. A disciple investor must be a person of *the* Book, the inspired, infallible, and inerrant Scriptures given to us through the ministry of the Holy Spirit. If you wish to survive in spiritual warfare (Ephesians 6:17), or to water (Psalm 1:1–3) and deepen the roots (Colossians 2:7) of your faith, you need to have a high view of and vibrant interaction with God's Word on a consistent basis. Not only do you believe it is God's Word (which is the disciple investor's starting point), but you read it, engage prayerfully with it, and use it in practical ways in your own life. As a matter of fact, you don't know how you can live without it! I once asked a professing believer, whom I knew possessed at least one readable version of the Bible, if he ever did read it. His reply was quite telling and certainly disappointing. He remarked, "No, but I pray a lot!" I am very glad that he prayed. I discovered a few years later that, like most Americans (believe it or not), although he is a college graduate from a premier educational institution, he doesn't like reading. Nevertheless, in time he began to practice ungodly habits and a lifestyle that would cause one to question his profession of faith in Christ. Possibly he is a Christian. But sadly, I can almost assure you that the truths of the Bible are not the foundation of his faith. Because he doesn't read the Bible, I'm not sure he even knows what the Bible says on many issues that address the Christian life. If you hope to invest in other disciples, you must have a high regard for God's Word. That is your starting point and it cannot be ignored.

## Bible Understanding

A commitment to the Bible as your life's foundation is your starting point, but growing in your understanding of the Scriptures is also necessary to be an effective disciple investor. I am not saying that you must be a Bible scholar or expert in order to disciple another person. Thankfully, disciple investing with young believers is usually premised on the reality that the other person is not as far along as you might be about understanding what the Bible actually says or teaches. Apparently today, biblical illiteracy in America is at an all-time high! He probably does know less than you know and he might actually think or perceive that *you* are a Bible expert if you start explaining whatever you do know (let's hope it's right, however)! And that reality is actually a primary source of joy and pleasure derived from the disciple investing process–you get to open up the Bible or teach biblical truths and watch the lightbulbs pop on! There is nothing more exciting than seeing another person discover new things about God, Christ, salvation, the Bible, and his own heart, while having his personal life changed by this new information. This is indeed the Holy Spirit's work and a marvel to behold–I have been blessed to see it happen many times over the years, both as a new believer and as a seasoned pastor. For the Christian, this experience is exhilarating!

But the possibility that you can actually watch God change another person's thinking, attitude, or life and behavior still brings us back to the fact that you need to know some things about the Bible. Therefore, although you don't need to be an expert, you do need to be a learner. Make it a personal goal to learn about Bible content or theology that you do not presently understand. Ask questions about your questions to someone who knows more than you. And when a younger believer asks questions that you cannot answer, be willing to simply say, "I don't know the answer to that!" But please add, "I will study that question and find an answer. Let's get together again to discuss it!" This is your opportunity to find the answer for yourself (as well as for him)! Growing and learning for your own benefit almost always precedes teaching others. Can you imagine if the person were to say, "I can't wait to know more about the answer to this question!" and, "You're going to help me? Thank you!" Pursue basic books, videos, blog posts/websites, or someone that is disciple investing in you that can teach you more about the answers to the question. Yes, you do have to be a learner on some level in order to help another person grow. We'll talk about that briefly when we discuss the "cost" of disciple investing. But, remember, *leading requires reading.* You don't have to be an expert, just willing to learn a little bit more than you previously knew. And that's not too hard, is it?!

## Questions for Reflection

1. How would you describe your walk with Christ? In what ways is it moving forward?

2. How is the Holy Spirit working in your life? What are some indications that he is?

3. In what ways have you seen God working in your life in such a way that you are battling with and/or overcoming specific sins in your life?

4. How does hypocrisy hinder a disciple investing relationship?

5. Which of the qualifications mentioned in this chapter are a strength in your life? Which might be a weakness? What can you do to grow in your weakness?

## Action Points

1. List the assets you have that would enhance friendship in a disciple investing relationship. How might you struggle to be a friend?

2. What personal changes or commitments can you make in your life in order to grow in your personal understanding of the Bible?

3. Can you think of someone who could help evaluate how you are doing in these areas of qualification? Who could assist you in your growth? As a name comes to mind, pursue the opportunity.

# 2

# Attitude

## The Essential Attribute of the Disciple Investor

IF, THUS FAR, WHILE reading this book, you have found yourself thinking that investing in the lives of other Christians (or even non-Christians) sounds like a potential opportunity to engage in life-changing experiences for both yourself and others, keep reading! One thing you have probably realized is that your *heart* truly needs to be immersed in this grand responsibility. Otherwise, how will you remain motivated to continue? This chapter could be considered something of an attitude check for your heart. We will try to answer the questions:

- "What attitudes do I need to be able to develop in order to assist in the spiritual progress of another individual?"
- "Has God done the work in my heart to enable me to be used by him to do his work in another person's heart?"

Let's explore our heart attitudes together.

### Gospel Driven

When we think of the message of the wonderful gospel, i.e., God's answer to our predicament of sin and fallenness, we can only think of the word "grace"! Grace is God gifting us with forgiveness and cleansing of sin, not due to our own merit and efforts, but by the work of Christ on the cross and that alone. It is undeserved merit. Grace cost Jesus both bodily and mental suffering, his shed blood, shame, and eventually an ignominious death. He experienced the wrath of the Father on behalf of his people and as a substitute for our sins. We can hardly fathom this wonder–it is unearthly and almost surreal. But God did it for us, and it is real! It moves us beyond words–we worship him in gratitude. And as we continue to understand the great love and patience that God has for us as sinners, and as we see the seemingly inexhaustible longsuffering and steadfastness he so often displays for his people (even when they constantly "blow it"), we begin to realize that God is a God of mercy and favor. To live out an understanding of God's grace in our lives is what is meant by being gospel driven. We wish to see holy obedience and growth in Christlikeness demonstrated in the disciple's life but we do not operate on a performance basis. We encourage, direct, guide, and love them. We call them to repent and follow the Lord. Being gospel driven means that, in relationship to the disciple, we keep ourselves from:

1) judgmentalism (a spirit of condemnation and overly negative criticism); 2) pressure to conform to our wishes; 3) legalistic or manmade expectations; and 4) moralism (doing good with false or non-God honoring motivations). We give the other person grace while yet calling him to respond to God's call and will in his life. We treat him with kindness, tenderheartedness, and forgiveness, just as God has forgiven us and treats us well in spite of our many acts of rebellion and unbelief (Ephesians 4:32). We are driven to express grace toward others because of the grace we have received.

## Love

The Christian life, and indeed the life of the disciple of Christ, is a life that resonates with love. As mentioned, when we looked at the Greatest Commandment above, first and foremost this love must be a deep love for the Lord. We love because he first loved us. Only when we comprehend God's love for us, a love that exists in spite of the fact that we were his enemies, ungodly sinners, and a love demonstrated through Christ's sacrifice on the cross, can we exude the love of God from our hearts toward others. The first fruit listed among the fruit of the Spirit is the fruit of love. As disciple investors, we must be motivated by love for those toward whom we are pouring out our lives. Love means commitment, sacrifice, and faithfulness.

And of course, the Apostle Paul writes that well known passage on love in 1 Corinthians:

> 4Love is patient and kind; love does not envy or boast; it is not arrogant 5 or rude. It does not insist on its own way; it is not irritable or resentful; 6 it does not rejoice at wrongdoing, but rejoices with the truth. 7 Love bears all things, believes all things, hopes all things, endures all things. 8 Love never ends.

How overwhelming is Christian or "agape" love! As we see, Paul never mentions feelings in the passage above. And although love may not be a "feeling," I would contend that we ought to have feelings of care and tenderness for those to whom we are ministering. We see this passionate care in the Apostle Paul when he addresses the wayward believers at Galatia, a congregation that was losing its grasp and grip on the crucial doctrine of justification by faith. Like a rejected parent, he cries out, ". . .my little children, for whom I am again in the anguish of childbirth until Christ is formed in you! I wish I could be present with you now and change my tone, for I am perplexed about you" (Galatians 4:19–20). For one who appears to be a rough and tumble itinerate apostolic messenger, ready even to die for the gospel, this man actually exudes personal anguish over these early believers in whom he had invested his life and teaching. How he wants them to become like Christ! Love for those in whom you are investing might not be easy, but it is absolutely necessary for the relationship to thrive for the long haul.

## Humility

Let's assume that you are working with someone who is a new believer, or a young but uninformed, believer in Christ. He doesn't know anything. God has dropped him into your lap, so to speak. Even with what you know or don't know, it is obvious that you can contribute to his understanding of God, Christ, salvation, the church, and how to follow Jesus. The temptation might exist (as mentioned above) to see yourself (or for him to see you) as the resident expert Christian scholar or authority, one to whom he should submit. In recent history, such opportunities for exerting "spiritual" authority have been expressed and radically abused. To be brief, in some Christian circles beginning in the early 1970s and into the eighties (I saw it at the University of Florida in 1981), a movement began which was known as "shepherding." The shepherding movement was exemplified by heavy and structured mentoring, a top-down approach in which a "more mature" or more knowledgeable believer would oversee a younger believer or disciple, while serving as the touch point for his/her every important decision. Ultimately, the perspective was, "I know the Lord well enough to tell you the Lord's will for your life."

If you understand what I am saying, then you will see that here is the key to what I am trying to espouse as the concept of "disciple investing." Remember: Jesus disciples his followers through his Spirit and uses you as only one element in the process. He is doing the work and using you. You are investing in the disciple's life and your goal is simply to be available, helpful, and a guide and counselor as the disciple learns how to follow Jesus. You personally hold no sway or authority over the other person (college students are the easiest to abuse, for multiple reasons) and should not even think in those terms. If there are any legitimate authority figures in the disciple's life, assuming that he has a church home or is a member of a church, that authority should be derived from acknowledged, or recognized (and preferably ordained) local church leadership. A posture of investing, i.e., looking to God and allowing him to work, demonstrates your reliance upon the Holy Spirit. Such a posture is opposed to an attitude of authority and mandating behavior. It involves a humility that acknowledges that not only are you not essential or necessary to the process of another's sanctification (growth as a Christian), but all you can contribute is that which has been given to you by God in the first place. I must mention my RUF campus mentor, Mark Lowrey, once more in this regard. He would always tell us as campus ministers, men with Master of Divinity degrees and schooled in some of the best of Reformed and evangelical seminaries, "When you spend time with students and try to teach them the Christian faith, always remember, you come as a fellow learner, learning from Jesus. You don't have all the answers!" That was great advice that I know we all needed to hear. Humble ministry is effective ministry and God will use you more when you realize that ultimately the work is his!

## Patience

One certainty about Christian growth is that it takes time. Sanctification (becoming more and more like Jesus) doesn't happen overnight. And it is not always clearly visible. We often want results while God is digging deeply into the vestiges of people's lives. We need to remember that we are dealing with people's hearts. Ironically, people's actions can change without heart change. Because of that, we do not always know what is truly going on inside. The disciple investor wonders, "Is anything happening in this person's life?" "Are my attempts to help her truly making a difference?" "Is change really occurring?" In some ways, all we can do is wait. Again, that is why consistency is a virtue in discipling others. As long as the other person is interested and willing, we keep showing up, keep trying, keep praying, and keep hoping that God will bring his fruit to bear on seemingly hard and impenetrable soil. God didn't change us overnight; therefore, we can learn to be more patient with the person that we are discipling. We must also be cognizant that God might be using other people or circumstances to reinforce whatever lessons or truths that we are trying to communicate. Remember that you are only investing in them; Jesus is discipling them in his own perfect way and time.

A few Christmases ago, I received a totally unexpected phone call from a former student from our RUF ministry in the 1980s. She had been involved in our ministry on a regular basis and both Cathy and I also met with her individually, as well as meeting with her as a couple, as she wrestled with the meaning of the Bible in her own life. We loved her and I believe that she loved us as well. However, eventually she moved on, graduated, and outside of one visit while passing through her home town, we lost contact. When this phone call occurred some twenty five years (or more) later, you can imagine that it was quite the surprise. She gave me a few updates on her life: she had gotten married and had a long term job and was quite successful in many ways. But then she proposed the reason for the call. She had come alive spiritually and in the past year or so, had given her all to the Lord. She wondered aloud why it took so long for her to make these realizations. "God wants all of me!" she said, and seemingly shaking her head on her end of the phone, she said, "I never knew how wonderful it could be to be 'all in' with Jesus!" She just had to call me and let me know that a transformation had happened in her life, and that Cathy's and my labors had not been in vain. Wow! I was and am still amazed at the faithfulness of God. Today I cannot explain why the Lord "waited" two and a half decades to break through to this friend and former student. He has his own timing and our times are in his hands. He works sovereignly and providentially–our role is to do our part and let him do his part, patiently waiting on his timing and his ways.

# A Listening Ear

Dietrich Bonhoeffer once stated,

> The first service that one owes to others. . .consists in listening to them. . . Many people are looking for an ear that will listen. They do not find it among Christians, because these Christians are talking when they should be listening. . . . Christians have forgotten that the ministry of listening has been committed to them by Him who is Himself the great listener and whose work they should share. We should listen with the ears of God that we may speak the Word of God.[1]

Similarly, Os Guiness, in his classic work, *Doubt*, writes, "To listen conveys more than any words. It says to the person in doubt: 'I am taking you seriously as a person. It matters to me that you are hurting. I am giving you myself if I can be any help.'"[2] Listening to others is a skill, an art and a discipline. It is a skill because everyone has potential to learn to listen and can improve their listening abilities (if they want to). It is an art because you have to learn how to listen to others, when to listen, and when not to speak. You need to know when to speak and not listen, and how to listen well. Listening well means listening carefully, attentively, and with the appropriate facial expressions and body language. You have to learn to listen in such a way that you perceive how the other person is painting a portrait through her conversational perspective. That is an art and one that can be more difficult than using the proper brush strokes with water colors on the canvas (I have no idea what I am talking about). Finally, listening is a discipline: it must be practiced in order to improve. It means restraint of the self and one's own self-expression. It means preventing your mind from roaming with other thoughts or quick retorts. It means secure eye contact, so that there is focus and minimal distraction on your part. The skill, art, and discipline of listening is imperative in the ministry of disciple investing. If listening also means love and help, it becomes mandatory on the part of the disciple investor. But, you might say . . . (ah, got you there, didn't I?). How big are your ears and how small is your mouth?

Some years ago, I came across the name of a man with whom I resonated. When I heard his name originally, I thought, "I must know more about him." Why? Because his last name was Culbertson. And, although

---

1. Dietrich Bonhoeffer, *Life Together* (New York: Harper and Row, 1954), 97–98.
2. Os Guiness, *Doubt* (Oxford: Lion Publisher Co., 1976), 150.

no longer living, he was still at least somewhat well known in the evangeli-cal Christian world. After doing some research, I discovered that for some twenty three years, he had been the president of Moody Bible Institute of Chicago. That fact alone endeared him to me, since I have always been fas-cinated with Mr. Dwight L. Moody, renowned evangelist in the latter half of the nineteenth-century, after whom the school is named. And then I read that this Culbertson was a Reformed Episcopal bishop, which was also amazing since Moody Bible Institute was not necessarily distinguished by either the Reformed or the Episcopalian traditions. I read that he was a very godly man and much respected, and those were encouraging facts as well. But the greatest lesson that I learned from Dr. William Culbertson (besides the fact that it is highly likely that I am at least distantly related to him) was one that had to do with listening. It is a lesson I will never forget and it changed my life ("though he died, he still speaks–Hebrews 11:4). I read that in every case, according to many personal testimonies, if you were speaking with William Culbertson, you would feel like you were the only person on the earth at that time. He would maintain eye contact, as well as his personal attention, upon you and you only, no matter what other distractions might be surfacing around you both. If you engaged in conversation with him, he was yours! So said the many people who knew him when he was living. Dr. William Culbertson was obviously a great listener and I think of him often when someone is speaking with or to me and I have distractions on my mind or all around me. As I said, he changed my life. And interestingly, as an anecdotal story (because this non-dynamic, characteristically calm but strong man is quite fascinating), when he died, he wasn't remembered for the art of listening. He spoke. His last words, as he gazed up toward the heavens, according to his successor at Moody, Dr. George Sweeting, who was at his bedside, were these, "Hallelujah, for the Lord God omnipotent reigneth" (from Revelation 19:6). And finally, "God, God. . .Yes!" And he was gone. The Great Listener of heaven, as Bonhoeffer would describe our God, heard his servant's final words, just before he entered his Lord's pres-ence. And what he listened to was exultant praise and confidence. So, can I ask you a question: "Can you become a listener for the sake of others?" I'm listening for your answer . . .

## Parenting: Fathering and Mothering

We have briefly discussed the fact that disciple investing parallels the role of parenting when we observed the Apostle Paul's grief, distress, and perplexity in watching the Galatian believers fall prey to insidious false teachers. No parents want to see their children deceived by those who operate in cult-like fashion. Thus, we understand that disciple investing with others carries not only a sense of responsibility, but also attitudes that reflect the way we truly feel about those who are providentially placed in our formative hands. In 1 Thessalonians 2:7–12, Paul writes,

> 7But we were gentle among you, like a nursing mother taking care of her own children. 8 So, being affectionately desirous of you, we were ready to share with you not only the gospel of God but also our own selves, because you had become very dear to us. 9 For you remember, brothers, our labor and toil: we worked night and day, that we might not be a burden to any of you, while we proclaimed to you the gospel of God. 10 You are witnesses, and God also, how holy and righteous and blameless was our conduct toward you believers. 11 For you know how, like a father with his children, 12 we exhorted each one of you and encouraged you and charged you to walk in a manner worthy of God, who calls you into his own kingdom and glory.

In this passage we observe a wonderful balance of pastoral or parental care: affection and exhortation. Here we see the Apostle Paul's appreciation for the distinctive roles that parents play in the lives of their children. In so many ways, disciple investing is very similar to child raising, even when the person leading the discipleship process has not been part of the disciple's spiritual "birthing" process. Paul is most definitely a type-A personality and a man's man who is willing to sacrifice his own life and body in the Christian "battle" as he proclaims the gospel. Yet, this feisty man is not only sensitive to the needs of others in his at-large ministry, but he describes his own ministry among the Thessalonican believers with "feminine" terminology. He uses words or phrases such as "mothering," even "nursing mother." He uses other terms like "gentle," "taking care," "child care," "affectionately," "desirous of you," "sharing our own selves," and "very dear to us."

Disciple investing obviously carries with it the concept of a sensitive, caring nature much like the constant awareness and attending nature of a small infant's or child's mother. I believe it is safe to say that, in observing the manly Apostle Paul's relationship to the believers in the church at

Thessalonica, one can build a case for feeling deeply on behalf of God's people. Disciple investing should unapologetically appear to be a form of mothering another person in the faith.

However, after using the "mothering" image, Paul doesn't stop there. Paul uses terminology that reflects a philosophy of "fathering" the follower of Christ as well. He becomes an advocate of full parenting. He uses the phrase, "like a father with his children," including in this concept words such as "exhorted," "encouraged," and "charged." And he indicates that his behavior is individualized ("each of you") with a goal that these believers might "walk in a manner worthy of God. . . " (1 Thessalonians 2:12)

When I was a young boy growing up, I fell in love with the game of baseball. I discovered that I was quite good at the game and began to play in both church and local city leagues. In my second year of Little League, I became the primary starting pitcher for the team. I loved the outfield but I could throw strikes, so a pitcher I became. My father was a former World War II Navy veteran and a product both of his generation as well as an uninvolved, strict father. He had never displayed much affection or interest in me during those first twelve years of life. But one day, he decided to attend one of my games. I must have had a good game (and I still remember my surprise at his attendance that afternoon), because afterward he decided that he would never miss another of my games, if at all possible. He realized, in that first viewing, that I had some talent. For the next six years, he came to as many of my games as possible.

However, probably the biggest embarrassment of my entire life occurred in one of the Little League games when he was in attendance. For some reason my mom was absent this day. We were winning a very tight game by one run against one of our better opponents, when, in the top of the sixth (the final inning), they got two men on base: first and second. Our coach (Herm "The Germ" Frazier) decided to bring me in from the outfield as a relief pitcher in order to stop the rally. The first batter I faced hit a soft grounder to our first baseman, drawing him far from the first base bag but not playable enough for him to throw to second base, or to get to first base and make the out himself. With great foresight and initiative, I quickly left the mound and ran to cover first base. The first baseman tossed the ball to me perfectly and we had an easy putout. I was rather proud of the play myself and many people were applauding. I felt like a major league pitcher in front of everyone. But, as I turned and looked at third to view the runner and assure myself that he would not run home behind my back, the runner, a rather aggravating friend and classmate of mine, starting hopping back and forth, as if he would run home on me. I knew he wouldn't dare run home but just to spook him a little, I pulled my throwing arm back, ball in hand, and then faked a hard throw toward third. That is when disaster struck. As I stopped my arm, the ball came out of my hand and rolled quickly between third and home. Chaos ensued.

My opponent friend ran toward home but the third baseman was quick enough to grab the ball and throw it to the catcher to put the runner in a rundown (or a "pickle," i.e., catching a runner between the bases, with throws back and forth). Feeling responsible for the situation and having a natural disposition to take control of every play on the field anyhow, I deftly got involved in the rundown. However, the third baseman threw the ball wildly past the catcher and as the catcher chased it to the backstop, I smartly covered home. He tossed me the ball, but just a little too late because the runner from third ran into me as I covered home plate. Worse yet, because I was terribly nearsighted, my black, horn rimmed glasses that I always wore to play went flying on the ground in one direction, while the ball went flying in the other direction. Of course, the next runner–the go ahead run–scored with very little effort, while I was picking myself up off the ground with dirt and dust covering me, no ball (or much else) to be seen anywhere. There was a lot of yelling from fans on both sides. I have to admit it was an exciting series of plays happening between competitive teams in a close game. Nevertheless, although I recovered from the ordeal and finished the inning with ease, we didn't score in our half of the final inning and we lost. It was quite discouraging and depressing, as you might imagine, for the psyche of a twelve year old. And here is the point.

After the game, both seeing and knowing my great dismay and grief at not only losing the game but being the very visible cause of the loss, my dad did something that was not only unusual (as in never before) but also uncharacteristic of him. And the timeliness of his act was both perfect and obviously memorable (the whole scene from fifty years ago remains vivid today). As I sat down on a fan bench outside of the field and the bulk of the crowd had dissipated, my father (who needed to get back to his law office, I'm sure) came over to me and took the time, albeit briefly, to do two things. First, he put his arm around me (he had never done that in my memory) in a consoling fashion and very gently cared for me like a mother. He was gentle, kind, and somewhat warm, which was not his style. I knew at that instance, as awkward as it really was, that my dad was interested in me beyond my skills on the baseball field. He was being very personal, showing that he cared for my feelings. Then, while consoling me, he spoke these memorable words that only a father could speak–and he spoke them with his strong, confident, fatherly tone: "I just want you to know that I overheard Coach Frazier talking about how the game ended, and he said to some of the other parents and fans, 'I would rather have Roddy Culbertson playing for me than anyone else in that situation. He is one of the best players on the team.'" What powerful, timely words those were (sometimes, I admit, I wonder if he made them up). The gentle motherly hug (if you wish to call it that) was one thing, but the encouraging and exhortative words were another. Put them together and you have an unforgettable childhood moment, one that I will cherish for the rest of my life. My dad, in my mother's absence, functioned for his son, in less than one minute's time, as both mother and father. And that is the idea in the task of disciple investing. If you are focusing your interest on the hopeful spiritual success of another believer, your attitude should be one of "apostolic" balance–I will mother and I will father; yes, I will parent this person with maternal and paternal instinct. Play Ball!

## Questions for Reflection

1. Give an example as to how these attitudes or approaches might hinder a gospel-driven disciple investing process:

    1) Judgmentalism: a spirit of condemnation and overly negative criticism

    2) Manipulation: pressure to make another person conform to our wishes

    3) Legalism: man-made expectations and rules of life

    4) Moralism: doing good with false/non-God honoring motivations

2. How does coming as a "fellow learner" enhance the disciple investing relationship?

3. Why is patience so crucial in the disciple investing process?

4. Compare and contrast the ministry styles of *mothering* and *fathering* another person.

## Action Point

1. Who do you know that might need a listening ear, or simply a conversation that would help you grow in the ministry of listening? How soon can you contact them to get together?

2. Is there a ministry or avenue in your church in which you can demonstrate love to others? Is there a way to call, visit, or send a card or note to someone who is grieving through a loss or rejoicing due to a victory?

# 3

## Cost

### Considerations on Your Part

NOTHING IN LIFE COMES easy, of course, and that is true even if you are just trying to live your own life while meeting normal daily responsibilities. I hope you are convinced that Jesus wants you to invest something of yourself and your time into another individual. Assuming that you are, be certain that there will be challenges, problems, personal strains, and demands upon the "normalcy" of your life. Life for you and the other individual(s) will become a little more complicated due to the requirements of coordinating your lives together, even if it is just to make plans to meet once a week or even once a month. The principle that must drive or govern disciple investing is the same word that should drive the Christian on a daily basis. Yet we all need to be reminded of this crucial word: sacrifice. Something will have to be sacrificed in the disciple investor's life. While there is a cost to this strategic ministry, I am fully convinced that the sacrifices you might make will be absolutely worth it. Therefore, as you consider your role in the disciple investing process, I want to mention a few aspects of the sacrificial costliness of the disciple investing enterprise.

## Being Equipped

Building a disciple investing relationship involves the "natural" building of any relationship, i.e., being spontaneous, hanging out together or having casual conversation, and time together. However, a vital disciple investing relationship includes intentionally discussing the role and implications of the Scriptures and the life of Christ in the disciple's life. To address someone's heart and life needs in this regard includes preparation. The disciple investor needs to take time to think and pray about the specific focus of the time with the disciple. Casual fun together is a positive activity, but if we are realists about the time that is available to point the other person toward Christ, we would easily recognize that we only have a few, fleeting moments to spend with them. Such a realization makes us more serious about how we spend our time together. We need to give due consideration to what we might read, study, or discuss with the disciple. And this type of preparation requires that we are equipped. Equipping requires that we ourselves have taken the time and energy to gain personal understanding of the issues. In chapter 1, we briefly discussed the need for biblical understanding in the mind of the disciple investor. You don't need to be a Bible scholar or expert, but you do need to be certain that you are equipped for the task. Being equipped might only mean that you have taken the time to learn more than the disciple in the given area of discussion. In chapter 8, I have provided a list of topics and Scripture passages that might help you in the process of disciple investing. To become better equipped might mean that at the very least, you choose a topic, read the relevant passage yourself, and then study the passage. You can become as equipped as you would like. You can create your own questions for discussion, read a commentary or online blog to understand the passage better, or speak to someone else who knows more than you do and gain their insights and help. All of these extra steps take time and are therefore costly. It might require giving up that special ball game on TV, missing the debut of the latest rage movie, or waking up a little earlier in the morning (or staying up later in the evening), or something similar. Being better equipped should actually be a very positive dimension in your own Christian life and growth; nevertheless, it will be costly.

## Time

The factor of time has already been alluded to in the previous discussion. Changing how you use your personal, discretionary and leisure time will certainly give you an added sense of the costliness of disciple investing. An hour per week easily becomes two hours, once you consider travel time and the likelihood that your conversation and discussion might easily slide into either extraneous flippancy, or deep and critical matters of concern. An hour–or a two-hour–long session per month is more conceivable, although meeting only once per month is not conducive to productive interchange. However, anything you can do with another person wanting to grow is profitable. I do believe that you can plan a scheduled single meeting that includes a set duration for that meeting and profit greatly by such structure. Of course, if you know your time is limited (because your focus becomes sharpened by the knowledge that your present time is precious) and there-fore precious, your focus becomes sharpened and you can expend your energies directly upon the subject or topic at hand. As a word of caution, I would add that if you have children, you should not sacrifice time raising your own children for a person outside of the family. Your children are your primary disciple investing responsibility when it comes to the use of your time. Nevertheless, it is possible for you to meet in your home with another individual, if he/she is willing, thus minimizing the time away from your child or children. No matter how you do it, time is still a heavy consider-ation and always remains a factor in one's commitment to invest in other disciples.

## Energy

As just mentioned in regard to time, working with another person includes exertion of extra energy and vitality on your part. Disciple investing means at least one less hour in your easy chair or on the couch; it means per-sonal exertion of both mental and emotional faculties; it means the possible stress of counseling and problem solving; and it means deliberate choices to go forward when you might be tired and exhausted. I really don't have to try to motivate you very much here because a look at Christ is all it takes:

> 1 Therefore, since we are surrounded by so great a cloud of wit-nesses, let us also lay aside every weight, and sin which clings so closely, and let us run with endurance the race that is set before us, 2 looking to Jesus, the founder and perfecter of our faith, who for the joy that was set before him endured the cross, despising the shame, and is seated at the right hand of the throne of God. 3 Con-sider him who endured from sinners such hostility against himself, so that you may not grow weary or fainthearted. 4 In your struggle against sin you have not yet resisted to the point of shedding your blood (Hebrews 12:1–4).

Enough said!

## Attention

Disciple investing requires a relational focus: the ability to watch out for another person on a regular basis. Those who are pastors or who have shepherds' hearts (often church elders and/or those who serve in the deacon role) understand what it means to give extra, or special, or regular attention to another person. The person doesn't necessarily have to have problems or extenuating circumstances; there is simply something about giving extra attention to the object of your affection. Adult children do this for aging parents all the time. But, whether there are problems or not, attention and focus will require both time and effort on the part of the disciple investor. In fact, attention normally surfaces previously unobserved and undiagnosed needs in the disciple's life, needs usually arising from either personal problems, self-destructive habits, or personal and self-defeating sins. The disciple investor makes her own personal commitment to care for the disciple and recognizes that such care is simply part of the mentality of disciple investing. Care for another (and this is a major element of disciple investing) necessitates attention, and attention is costly for the one who gives it! Please give that thought some attention!

## Follow-up

The concept of attention indicates focus and concern, as opposed to inattentiveness. If giving attention to another appears a bit intimidating, then giving attention for the long haul (or to the unresponsive) will most probably be even more intimidating. This form of attention eventually can become more strenuous and requires more effort because it means deliberately seeking, inquiring, and sometimes pursuing and constantly initiating on the part of the disciple investor. Follow-up of this sort is the pursuit of the other person in a manner that lets her know that we are seriously interested in her welfare. Ours is not a temporary or flighty form of attention and a lack of responsiveness will be countered by assertive love on our part. Follow-up with another person, after she has displayed initial interest or after initial interest seems to have waned or subsided, should never appear as an overbearing, pressurized, manipulative, or obligatory task. The disciple investor trusts a sovereign God to bless her efforts and she goes in faith hoping for a Holy Spirit-prepared response.

## The Five "I's" of Investment

Finally, I would like to briefly address five progressive and interrelated concepts that are connected to the nature of the costliness of disciple investing. I call them "The Five "I's" of Investment."

1.  Interest–Every relationship begins with interest on the part of one or both parties, and the disciple investing relationship is no different. Although there may be multiple possible motivations, good or bad, for reaching out to a person as a potential disciple (guilt, pity, self-exaltation or self-gratification, helpfulness, team building, and co-dependence, etc.), the primary and premier motivation for expressing, initiating, and promoting a disciple investing relationship is that of love. The love of God cuts through all other motivations and provides the constant source of patient, persistent interest in the other person. If you as the disciple investor demonstrate unconditional love for the other person, putting up with foibles, sins and failures, mutual interest can be maintained and will flourish in time. People want to know you care for them and showing sincere and genuine personal interest is the place to start. The cost of disciple investing is minimized if true love and interest prevails.

2.  Ideas–Interest is the starting point but then the disciple investor must come up with ideas of how to find, reach, and begin ministering to the other person. Ideas are the creative element of the process but one doesn't have to be too creative. Just look for where people congregate and become a little sociable yourself. The disciple investor can meet people at church, ask the pastor if he has any leads or knows open individuals, attend church events and social gatherings or branch out to places outside of the church, such as fitness clubs, PTA meetings and children's sports, as well as other team loyalties or events where either participation or being a fan unites you to others. The list of ideas could be as endless as the creativity of the person thinking them through.

3.  Intention and Initiative–Ideas are wonderful but they are meaningless if not carried forth. The disciple investor must find the motivation to act upon whatever leading she has to meet or initiate contact with

other people. She must tell herself, "This is a good idea. Now, what do I do about it and when do I start?" She must plan a date, time, and locale for getting started. Again, it could be as simple as asking her church pastor or youth director if either one of them has people in mind with whom she could start a discipling relationship. Church staff would probably be thrilled to know that someone has intentions like these. Or she could set out to visit the numerous meetings, church events or other Christian ministry events available in the community, if applicable. Initiative, initiative, initiative. That is intention being acted out.

4. Implementation–Once the disciple investor declares his intentions to himself, then he must make something happen. He must find the person or persons with whom to meet and must determine a definite time and place to begin meeting. He must explain what his hopes and plans might be for the purpose of the meetings. He can decide to emphasize a walk-through as well as discussion of a particular book of the Bible, or to read a significant book written by a reputable and solid Christian author (or an appropriate non-Christian author) also for discussion, or to choose a topic (or topics) of discussion that can be scripturally addressed. Or together disciple investor and disciple can meet with a few others using the same strategy above. Something must be planned and done–the good intentions must be implemented. Again, outside help (from church pastor, staff, an experienced lay person or someone else in ministry) can help the disciple investor through both guidance and accountability. Just do it!

5. Involvement–I add this category or stage simply to say that once the disciple investor does implement his ideas and the meetings begin, it is the nature of ministry to require involvement in the other person's life. This is not only attending basic meetings with the other person, or doing casual get-togethers or social events, but in time, the disciple investor becomes an involved participant in the other person's successes, failures, struggles, joys, sorrows, and problems. As the disciple investor's heart becomes intertwined with that of the disciple, and actually because of the love of Christ in your heart for this individual you would have it no other way. You have been watching the Lord work in your mutual relationship from the beginning stage (the "interest" in or love for them) and the other person or persons have become part of who you are. To put it simply, your involvement goes well beyond just

involvement–your lives are meshed, Christ is present in your midst and whatever happens, good or bad, is shared between you. Disciple investing, seen in this light, is a costly investment but well worth all of the expenditure mandated by the interest, the ideas, the initiative/ intention, the implementation, and the involvement. Most of the time there are no regrets!

## Questions for Reflection

1. What are some activities in your life that you could curtail or shorten in order to find more time to study the Bible and become better equipped in using it in the ministry of another's life?

2. Which do you think is more challenging in the disciple investing ministry–finding the *time* or maintaining the *energy* required to continue a regular relationship?

3. What do you think would be both the blessings and the struggles in the process of "follow up" with another person?

4. What type of problems needing attention might surface in the life of another that could concern you in regard to investing in her life?

5. What are some of the personal hurdles of a disciple investor's life that might prevent him from pursuing any or all of the "Five I's" listed at the end of this chapter?

## Action Points

1. Purchase a commentary or a book that you could read to study or better understand the Bible.

2. Do some research to see what websites, blogs or other ministries you might subscribe to in order to receive a regular, informative, and thoughtful means of biblically equipping yourself.

# 4

## Direction
### Principles of Disciple Investing

PROBABLY THE BIGGEST FEAR or concern for someone interested in pouring one's life into, or at least contributing to, the spiritual life of another person in a focused (and seemingly intense) manner is wondering with whom we should "partner." We wonder, "How do you find someone who needs me or wants to receive my input in his/her life?" I can assure you that, without quoting quite a few studies or surveys, there are a number of people in either your world, or most certainly in your church, who would be open to having someone help them in their walk with Christ. Sometimes they don't even understand what they need but would be open to someone else's initiative to move in the direction of a spiritual relationship. I teach a discipleship class at Reformed Theological Seminary which is offered every two years as an elective. Because it is an elective, the class enrollment is not very large. Nevertheless, when I start the course, on the first day of class, I ask the students who are enrolled, "How many of you have ever had another Christian disciple you in an intentional effort and probably in a one-to-one fashion?" Most often, all of the students in attendance affirm that not only did someone invest in their lives spiritually in a focused manner, but that they are both grateful for the disciple investor's interest in them personally and still in close relationship with that person. I say all that to underscore that there are people that are available for disciple investing, and they only need someone to ask about their interest in being discipled. Just think of the teenager, the college student, the early career friend, the single man

29

or woman, the millennial, the disenfranchised, and countless others who would appreciate someone coming along as a discipler or a mentor or a friend who will help them grow. Pray and look around.

So, how do you find the right person or people? Here are some thoughts.

## Jesus's Method

As mentioned in the introduction, my approach to both kingdom building and disciple investing was very heavily influenced while I was in college at the University of South Carolina. But although I was impacted by the Navigator ministry in which I was involved, and also by my lengthy tenure in Campus Crusade for Christ (Cru), the life-changing influence that I personally experienced in this regard came from reading a book. That book was written by a seminary professor, Dr. Robert E. Coleman, and entitled, *The Master Plan of Evangelism.* Divided into eight succinct chapters and based primarily on the New Testament Gospel accounts, the basic premise of the book is that disciples of Christ are made by taking significant time to invest in them as individuals, rather than simply focusing upon large numbers or the masses (contrary to how we usually think in our western culture).

Coleman also makes a pivotal suggestion, one that requires a faith leap on the part of anyone involved in the disciple investing process: the discipler must recognize that the efforts put into investing in others may not bear fruit until years later. It is not the present results that count, but the future product and fruitfulness (the work that God does and that the discipler often never sees) that a disciple investor must consider when placing time, energy, and relational effort into building disciples for the kingdom. Jesus had only one plan to reach the world with the news of the kingdom of heaven, and that plan was to entrust its success into the hands of a small group of inadequate men. Such an approach is profound, as it seems improbable. Ultimately, Jesus selected, associated with, led, taught, mentored, and delegated his work and vision to a handful of men (men who might be termed "suspect") and then left them behind to reproduce all that he had taught them and given them. The rest is history.

## One Person Can Change the World

*The Master Plan of Evangelism* will challenge the disciple investor to think through the question, "In whom am I directly investing so that they might know Christ better?" Don't be deceived by numbers. Rather, assess ministry success by judging the reality of Christ-likeness in the lives of those who name the name of Christ. That premise is the beauty of Coleman's book. Upon reading *The Master Plan of Evangelism* the first time, I realized that ministry numbers were not always indicative of spiritual realities. I had to ponder and pray deeply and ask the question, "What really matters in ministry?" *The Master Plan* helped me answer that question simply by looking at what really matters to Jesus and what ultimately matters to God, i.e., individual heart transformation. Such heart transformation is derived from honestly dealing with the Scriptures in a context of pouring oneself into others. This is how one person can help change the world and build Christ's kingdom on earth. What was it that I bought into from *The Master Plan*? I will never forget this convincing statement:

> Here is where we must begin just like Jesus. It will be slow, tedious, painful, and probably unnoticed by men at first, but the end result will be glorious–even if we don't live to see it. Seen in this way, though, it becomes a big decision in ministry. One must decide where he wants his ministry to count–in the momentary applause of popular recognition, or in the reproduction of his life in a few chosen men who will carry on his work after he has gone. Really, it is a question of which generation we are living for.[1]

As a senior college student, I bought into Dr. Coleman's conclusions, that Jesus builds his kingdom through personal, intensive investment in a few. I realized that whatever I do in ministry (and I was not yet called to full-time, lifetime ministry at the time), even if it is small, is important to God. Also, any effort I might give to other individuals to help move them closer to the Lord and toward Christ-likeness is consequential. I did not conclude that numbers are meaningless (the book of Acts is a testament to the undeniable, significant growth of the early church) but statistics need to be kept in their place and in perspective.

---

1. Robert Coleman, *The Master Plan of Evangelism* (Grand Rapids: F.H. Revell, 1963), 37.

## Managing Individual Meetings

For a moment, I want to visit *The Master Plan of Evangelism* once more. If I believe that investing in a smaller group of people was (at least potentially) more strategic than investing in a large group of people, how might this work out in the local church? The reality is that in the local church, meeting times with men can be limited due to busy work schedules, family priorities, and commitments. We have to ask the obvious questions about the one or those in whom we hope to invest ourselves. With whom do we meet? Who is our priority? How do we spend our time? When it comes to meeting with men, I discovered that I could meet with most working men either for breakfast most any weekday morning, or possibly lunch most weekdays, or maybe late afternoon, depending upon their job, or Saturday mornings if my children didn't have their numerous sports activities at that time. Professional working women will have to make similar considerations. Women who are primarily at home or mothers can certainly use their homes, depending upon the schedules and needs of their children, but might find more flexibility than most working women in meeting with other mothers or other women in general.

## Selecting a "Disciple"

From Dr. Coleman's book, I had indeed become convinced that the first step in discipling other men, as Jesus demonstrated, was "selection." Jesus chose certain men to be his followers. And he told his twelve disciples, "You did not choose me, but I chose you and appointed you that you should go and bear fruit and that your fruit should abide, so that whatever you ask the Father in my name, he may give it to you." (John 15:16) Using wisdom and insight (that he willingly grants to us as well), Jesus chose twelve men to be his closest followers and out of those, he chose three to whom he gave what we might call special preference. Dr. Coleman writes, ". . .the more concentrated the size of the group being taught, the greater opportunity for effective instruction." (27) Of course, I have been proposing that you, the reader, should think in terms of finding just one, or as many as three in whom to invest. But seeking someone in whom to invest is crucial and selection is pivotal in the process. And as always, remember to pray about your selection, as Jesus did when he choose the twelve (Matthew 9:36–10:4).

## Criteria for Selection

How should you select the person or people with whom you might work? Here are a few helpful answers based on *my* practices and experiences:

1. Much of the "choosing" was natural and based on the use of sanctified common sense. I usually looked for people in whom God was obviously working.

2. I looked for those who were growing in the Lord.

3. I looked for people who were willing to learn, listen, and be taught.

4. I looked for someone who would have the time to meet with me and not become too busy or distracted by other priorities. That is a hard quality to judge.

5. Often, I would become interested in a person who had potential because I had observed how he was responding to God's Word in his life.

6. If he had a relationship to the local church but appeared disconnected to or wasn't joining in with others, he might have potential. He's "there," but isn't being helped.

7. I looked for relational chemistry, i.e., someone who related well to me/others.

8. I looked for some measure of humility, even if the person was feisty (I usually like feisty; you may not). The proud and self-sufficient are often simply too difficult and non-cooperative as someone with whom to work.

9. I looked for those who were sensitive to the Lord's will. This attribute was crucial. I myself am a skeptic and battle cynicism and know that such an attitude can be debilitating in a learning and relational context. The desire to ultimately do the Lord's will, no matter what he requires, is a picture of a person submitted to the Lordship of Christ.

## Paul's Principles

The Apostle Paul was a stellar example of disciple investing, as it seems that everywhere he went, he found others to influence. It would be wise to consider the example and practices of the Apostle Paul, who was the first century paragon model of disciple investing and leadership training.

A study of Paul's methods should assist us in understanding some practical lessons for disciple investing. We can observe Paul's practice, as recorded in the New Testament in the following ways:

## Personal Communication

Paul is an activity-driven individual, but he nevertheless maintains an emphasis on *personal communication* in his disciple investing. We see this, of course, in his correspondence and letters (epistles) to various churches and individuals. The bottom line lesson here is that Paul stays in touch with people and those he cares about. Such letters often reflect that Paul wants to keep the lines of communication open; he wishes to follow up with churches and individuals to see how they are doing. He wants to problem solve and he wants to maintain openness and awareness of his own needs and the needs of others. We need to make conversation and communication with our disciples our priority, and to keep the lines of communication open. Transparency, honesty, and openness must prevail. Often, in order to maintain this commitment, the initiative must be ours, not theirs.

## Personal Time, Attention, and Focus

Although often viewed as a man on the move, if one looks at his journeys in the latter half of the book of Acts, we discover that the Apostle Paul spends three years in the city of Ephesus. His personal time there and the attention and focus that he gives to these believers bears obvious fruit. Elsewhere we see the commitment that the Apostle has to being with people, particularly those who are converted through or influenced by his ministry. Paul's desire to spend time with new converts in particular is very evident from a study of the book of Acts.

## Personal Sacrifice

A constant theme in the Apostle Paul's ministry is that of dying to self. He is a man willing to sacrifice himself and his creature comforts because he knows that Christ sacrificed himself for the Apostle: ". . .who loved me and gave himself *for me*" (Galatians 2:20, emphasis mine, based upon Paul's obvious personal application). We reflect soberly on his expressions of suffering, recognizing that he endures much for the ministry of proclamation and investment. As Dietrich Bonhoeffer states, being a disciple is costly. We might add, based on Paul's own testimony, that disciple investing is costly as well. We must constantly recognize that disciple investing will include personal sacrifice on our part.

## Personal Example

Paul convincingly believes in the great value of *personal* example. Although he includes numerous references to his emphasis on being exemplary, I quote only one from 1 Corinthians 11:1, "Be imitators of me, as I am of Christ." Paul understands that although ultimately the disciple or the believer must pursue the Spirit-filled Christian life by fully following Christ, their Lord and Savior, a natural human-to-human influence nevertheless exists. The older convert and mature believer can exert a great impact upon newer, fledgling believers. The call to holiness and assertive Christian growth and maturity (actively using the means of grace) spawned by a proper understanding of God's grace lends itself to a Christ-like, exemplary Christian lifestyle, a lifestyle with potential for emulation. Personal example is a powerful teacher; thus the disciple investor, without question, will instruct others by his own life and practice.

## Praise

In 2 Corinthians 9:1–2, we read, "Now it is superfluous for me to write to you about the ministry for the saints, 2 for I know your readiness, of which I boast about you to the people of Macedonia, saying that Achaia has been ready since last year. And your zeal has stirred up most of them . . ." In this Scripture, we clearly see that when Paul observes laudable behavior among the churches with which he has worked, he is pleased to commend them. The need for properly attributed praise, whether in written or in verbal form, cannot be underestimated. Paul fully understands that good works flow from God's work. But when he sees the works flowing out of his disciples' lives, he gladly affirms them in writing. Whether blessed with the *gift* of encouragement or not, the disciple investor should make every effort to note and properly praise the progress seen in the disciple's life. Sin is too destructive and spiritual progress is too slow and arduous for any positive change to go unnoticed or unmentioned. The disciple investor must use the ministry of praise discerningly in the lives of Christ's followers and ultimately, God will receive the glory!

## Prayer

The Apostle Paul cherished the believers in the church at Philippi and when he writes to them, he lets them know that the depths of his feelings drive him toward prayer on their behalf. His first few written words expresses this fact, "I thank my God in all my remembrance of you, 4 always in every prayer of mine for you all making my prayer with joy, 5 because of your partnership in the gospel from the first day until now." (Philippians 1:3–5). The declaration of thanks to God for the effects of gospel proclamation reverberates from Paul's communications as a constant stream. He knows that his work and the fruit of that work have their origins in the gracious hand of God. I believe that disciple investing can easily fall prey to fleshly effort and accomplishment, forgetting that the Holy Spirit is the source of all ultimate spiritual change. Constant and frequent prayer must become the salve that is applied to the deep spiritual needs of God's people in order for them to continue to grow, heal, and respond to God's Spirit. The disciple investor must pray for his own efforts, that they might be blessed by God's hand, and must also pray earnestly for those for whom he is expending such effort.

## Principle of Mutuality

In this rather obscure and often overlooked passage Paul writes, "I rejoice at the coming of Stephanas and Fortunatus and Achaicus, because they have made up for your absence, 18 for they refreshed my spirit as well as yours. Give recognition to such people." (1 Corinthians 16:17–18) With these remarks, Paul joyfully declares the benefits of receiving the favorable presence of others in his life. As we pause and contemplate Paul's words, we see something beautiful about the disciple investing process. The process is not simply a one-way street or a top-down exchange. Although the disciple investor is assumed to be more spiritually mature and has made more progress in the Christian walk than the disciple, it appears, from the Apostle Paul's description, that the more mature believer (even an Apostle) can be mutually ministered to by his followers. Stephanas, Fortunatus and

Achaicus, three truly unknown New Testament personalities provide Paul with a refreshed spirit, a strong ministry in his life.

The "principle of mutuality" proposes that the disciple investor will inevitably benefit in multiple ways by the relationship he has with the growing disciple. Growing disciples demonstrate enthusiasm and zeal for the things of God, attitudes that might have waned somewhat over time in the life of the disciple investor. Growing disciples ask hard questions, raising issues that challenge the disciple investor and cause him to pursue the Lord or his understanding of the Lord in a greater way. Like the Apostle Paul's experience, the growing disciple may contribute in some fashion to the needs of the disciple investor, bringing him glimmers of joy, comfort, or encouragement. Growing disciples can often contribute perspective from past experiences that are different from those of the disciple investor and that helps the disciple investor to apply his knowledge of Scripture and God to new areas of life. When a maturing believer invests in another believer's growing life, the benefits are often mutual: both of them grow individually, even as they grow together.

## Positive Attitude in Christ

Paul's letter to the Philippians is a book that radiates and is filled with joy. He remains upbeat in the midst of the early trials of his ministry. Of course, ultimately Paul's joy is derived from his confident relationship with the risen Christ. Jesus is with Paul in his imprisonment, in this case, as he is under house arrest. Here is a man suffering opposition and yet he can write in his closing exhortations, "Rejoice in the Lord always; again I will say, rejoice." (4:4) Other sample verses written earlier in the book (1:3–4, 18) display Paul's positive exhortations and demonstrations of joy in the face of adversity and even life threatening situations. The attitude of the disciple investor is key to her work with the disciple. Exemplifying a radiant joy and confidence in the Lord in the midst of daily struggles brings great benefit to those with whom she works. The disciple observes the positive expressions of faith that deep trust in the Lord brings to the disciple investor, and gains a natural encouragement as she faces her own trials.

## Preaching/Teaching

The most obvious means that Paul uses to build up and invest in other believers and to reach unbelievers is *teaching and preaching*. Communicating both the gospel and the truths of Scripture is the necessary ministry of disciple investing. Teaching, of course, occurs all the time in one-to-one relationships and this is why we open up the Word of God with another individual: so that we can be taught by the Holy Spirit. If you do not feel qualified to teach, remember the advice given earlier: study what you can and share what you have learned with the disciple.

## Organic Means Helpful

One consideration that I would like to mention briefly is that of context. Context defines the setting in which you are investing in the disciple. Sometimes you meet the individual in a work office, through a neighborhood connection, a health club or gym-type environment, a local school or civic committee, etc. and the context is not very strategic to disciple investing outside of one-to-one efforts. Other times, you meet the potential disciple in relationship to a small group in your church or some other ministry, like a parachurch men's, women's, singles', or career ministry. Such a group can be a very beneficial context. Then, often, as the most natural context, you meet the individual in a large group setting, such as a church worship service, a church social or outreach gathering, or some other ministry setting in which a large number of people are attending. Depending upon the nature of that large group, as well as its function, that can be a great context to invest in another person's life.

My basic premise in the concept of "disciple investing" is that *you* are not necessarily the "critical" piece or most necessary factor in the disciple investing process. You are just one element that Jesus is using to disciple the other person. It encourages us to know that there are very many other factors and people to help hold the responsibility for the disciple's growth. This is why context is so important. I believe that (despite her frequent failures and weaknesses) the local church is the most effective "context" for disciple investing. All of the benefits that the local church has to offer–corporate worship, the sacraments, the preaching of the word, the fellowship of other believers, church teaching, service opportunities, friendships, church officers and oversight, personal support, and rebuke–all contribute to the life and health of the disciple. All of these factors combine together in the sense of influence, and act as a complement to your efforts with the disciple. They could be termed the "organic" nature of church life. These organic influences assist whatever efforts you contribute to the growth of the disciple and take some of the pressure off of you. Small group involvement has potential to be organic in nature as well, although in reality a small group ministry or influence is only part of the more powerful large group organic impact, as used by the Holy Spirit. I truly believe that we do not and never will fully understand the unseen impact of the organic nature of the local church in the life of a believer. But God is working through the means of grace and among his people to help the disciple grow spiritually. Your efforts are also a part of the process. Organic growth is helpful to individual growth and God uses it to work in all of his children's lives!

## Questions for Reflection

1. Who can you think of that has invested substantially in your own walk with Christ? What is your relationship with them today?

2. Why does "choosing" another person with whom to work seem uncomfortable? Why does it seem important to "select" him/her?

3. Which of the "Principles of Paul" is most appealing to you personally? Which might best match your personality or style? Why?

4. What do you think of the "organic" dimension of disciple investing and how is it positive?

## Action Points

1. Managing your schedule: consider what might be the best times in your personal schedule that would work for you in meeting with another person on a regular basis. What do you have to do to make it work?

2. List some people groups where you can find someone in whom to disciple invest.

# 5

## Focus

### Outcomes–What Does a Disciple Look Like?

THUS FAR, WE HAVE defined the ministry of discipleship, or "disciple investing" as I prefer to call it, and we have also considered the qualifications and
attitudes of, as well as the cost to, the disciple investor (you, I hope). Now,
we must consider what a disciple of Christ looks like in today's world. What
are the attributes of a person who is following Jesus Christ as Lord and
growing to become more and more like him? What outcomes do we, as disciple investors, hope and look for? Naturally, the categories and measure-
ments for this assessment could be innumerable. But I would like to select
a manageable number of attributes of a follower of Jesus to contemplate.
Let's cover the basic qualities that one should be able to observe in the life of
the growing believer. We will look briefly at twenty distinct attributes that
ought to be evident in any follower of Jesus today.

### What Are the Attributes of a Disciple: Recognizing a Disciple of Jesus

Conversion brings change. The change in the life of the new believer is
known as sanctification. The great Reformed doctrinal summary known as
the Westminster Shorter Catechism defines sanctification as "the work of
God's free grace, whereby we are renewed in the whole man [person] after
the image of God, and are enabled more and more to die unto sin and live

unto righteousness." (Q.35) A new believer in Christ will exhibit change, even while the old nature continues to manifest itself, sometimes in very ugly ways. But these changes are a great encouragement to the souls of both the disciple and the disciple investor, as she sees some of the fruit of her labors.

1. Demonstrates Love–As mentioned earlier, the first fruit listed among the fruit of the Spirit is the fruit of love. This beautiful fruit begins to mature when Christ enters a person's life. Romans 5:5 states, "and hope does not put us to shame, because God's love has been poured out into our hearts through the Holy Spirit, who has been given to us." In so many ways the person who has lived life without Christ has lived life for self. Any semblance of self-love ruins a good work in God's eyes because the motivation is impure. Conversion to Christ is an experience of God's great love and out of that new life flows a new and growing love. "This is my commandment, that you love one another as I have loved you. 13 Greater love has no one than this, that someone lay down his life for his friends." (John 15:12–13) Sacrificial and committed "agape" love for others is a sign that an individual is a disciple and follower of Jesus, the one who gave his life for us. This love is a sure evidence of a changed and obedient believer!

2. Lives to Glorify God–Ultimately, this disciple can answer the questions, "Who (or what) is first in my life?" and, "Why do I exist?" These questions address what is often called "The Lordship Commitment." Does Christ hold first place in the life of the disciple? Will she submit to and obey his revealed will in all matters of life? Is her passion and motivation now upon glorifying God instead of living for self? The Apostle Paul told the believers at Corinth (who truly struggled with their passions), "So, whether you eat or drink, or whatever you do, do all to the glory of God." (1 Corinthians 10:31) The growing disciple begins to discover areas of her personal life that need to be submitted to the will of Christ. She wants to live for God's glory and not for herself. Self is no longer the driving force in a believer's life.

3. Grows in Christ-likeness–After I became a Christian, the first verse that I memorized was from the Navigator Topical Memory System (TMS). For me, it was absolutely true, "Therefore, if any man be in Christ, he is a new creature: old things are passed away; behold all things are become new!" (KJV) The believer in Christ is changed. He

realizes that his motto in the Christian life could easily be patterned after the words of John the Baptist when he states, "He must increase, but I must decrease." (John 3:30) The disciple of Christ wants to become more like Christ and less like self. Through the use of the means of grace (Scripture, prayer, the sacraments, worship and fellowship, etc.), he finds that only a life that is conforming to Christ-likeness will satisfy. Each disciple of Christ willingly asks the question of himself, "Am I becoming more and more like Jesus in my attitudes, actions, choices, and lifestyle?"

4. Lives Obediently–As mentioned previously in the description of "lives to glorify God" above, the growing disciple of Christ has a new standard for her life. She wants to know what God says through his word and wants to do what she hears God say. This life of obedience, lived by the Spirit and out of gratitude for God's grace, is a proof of love for Jesus, "As the Father has loved me, so have I loved you. Abide in my love. 10 If you keep my commandments, you will abide in my love, just as I have kept my Father's commandments and abide in his love. 11 These things I have spoken to you, that my joy may be in you, and that your joy may be full." (John 15:9–11) Learning submission to the will of God is a true sign that one is a child of God. The Apostle Paul "kicked against the goads" and it took a Damascus Road crisis to bring him into full submission. He also discovered a zealous enthusiasm to suffer whatever cost and demands were required to live for, as well as to proclaim, Christ. Living under grace means that the disciple strives to please the Lord. She does not abuse grace in such a way to live a life of license (freedom to sin). She learns to love the thought of obeying the One she follows with all she has!

5. Grows in Holiness–The disciple of Christ has a new attitude toward his personal sin. Others' sins might bother him and society's ills might be personally discouraging and inflaming, but suddenly he sees that the biggest problem in the entire world is his own sin. Like David, he cries out, "For I know my transgressions, and my sin is ever before me. 4 Against you, you only, have I sinned and done what is evil in your sight, so that you may be justified in your words and blameless in your judgment." (Psalm 51:3–4) Usually, the sensitivity to personal sin becomes enormous. As a matter of fact, on a number of occasions, I have heard young believers bemoan the fact that they didn't realize that they had so much sin in their lives. Others have stated that they

were happier as non-Christians because they could sin and not feel so badly or be convicted by it. The growing disciple hates his sin. He begins to acknowledge it more readily. He begins to think, "I have more sin than I thought I did. I didn't know that I could sin so much." Holiness involves dying to sin and living for righteousness (1 Peter 2:24). Growth in holiness means "putting sin to death" and seeking all the means necessary to live for Christ. As the believer recognizes that he is secure "in Christ," he is able to pursue holiness without which no one will see the Lord (Hebrews 12:14). He knows that Christ is his victory and failure is not the end. He loves the law as a means to guide him in a life that is pleasing to God. He wants to be holy as God is holy (1 Peter 1:14–15).

6. Loves Truth and *the* Truth–The new believer begins to understand the words that Jesus spoke to the Jews of his day, "If you abide in my word, you are truly my disciples, 32 and you will know the truth, and the truth will set you free" (John 8:31b-32). She has discovered that God's Word is truth and she agrees with Jesus when he prayed, "Sanctify them in the truth; your word is truth" (John 17:17). She now knows that God's word is true and the means to change her heart and life. And not only does she value truth, she realizes that instead of living in a world of lies, she now must make integrity and honesty a defining mark of her walk with God. God knows all, sees all, and calls his people to a life of truthfulness. The ninth commandment states, "You shall not give false testimony against your neighbor." She now wishes to hear truth, believe truth, love truth, and live truthfully and honestly. The lies and hypocrisy shall be no more!

7. Walks by Faith, Not by Feelings–God's people should indeed "walk by faith, not by sight" (2 Corinthians 5:7). And we cannot walk by feelings either, although the presence of feelings and emotions about the Lord are not to be dismissed as inappropriate in the Christian life. As we first trusted Christ for our salvation from sin and hell, so we must continue to trust the Lord through our entire lives. "This is the victory that has overcome the world–our faith." (1 John 5:4) The disciple of Christ learns to trust God through the good and the bad, during the blessings and the trials. In his prayer life, the disciple is able to express desires and hopes and to cast his every care and worry upon the Lord because he cares for us (1 Peter 5:7). As growing disciples, we gradually learn that God has a plan for us and that he also has the

power to provide for us. And he answers prayer. We can give him our worries (Luke 12:22–26) and our future (Matthew 6:34) as he knows every need of our lives (Matthew 6:25–34). The disciple lives a life of faith even when the feelings and the sense of the presence of God is missing. This is the walk of faith: trusting God when all that you can see about the future is that it is in God's hands.

8. Lives Sacrificially–Eventually a growing disciple realizes that not only does Christ call his followers to deny themselves, take up their cross and follow him (Luke 9:23), but he also calls them to live sacrificially. The self-life must die and Christ must live. Christ himself was a sacrifice for us. Paul writes, "I appeal to you therefore, brothers, by the mercies of God, to present your bodies as a living sacrifice, holy and acceptable to God, which is your spiritual worship" (Romans 12:1). In daily living, believers are to sacrifice themselves as an act of worship. Giving up ourselves, our possessions, our time, our personal rights, and perceived privileges should be part of the Christian life. Each disciple must understand the will of the Lord in such personal matters and decisions, and must ask himself, "What am I giving up in order to serve Christ and help fulfill the Great Commission?" C.T. Studd, the missionary pioneer to Belgian Congo in the early 1900s, once made this compelling statement, "If Jesus Christ be God and died for me, then no sacrifice can be too great for me to make for him."[1] A growing disciple is sensitive to what he can give up for the Savior who gave himself for his own.

9. Repents Constantly–This concept relates to the area above designated as "Grows in Holiness." The disciple of Christ becomes sensitive to sin, sees more sin than ever before in his life, hates the sin more, and therefore learns to repent daily (if not momentarily) as a way of life. Confession and repentance are absolutely essential for living a life of victory in the Christian life. Once the believer becomes aware of sin, he must acknowledge it with honest introspection, confess it before the Lord, give thanks that Christ has paid for and covered the sin and then with wholehearted resolve, turn from the sin. Failure in the Christian life is inevitable. Nevertheless, Satan will get the upper hand if the believer doesn't abhor his sin, grieve over it (as the Holy Spirit grieves over it), and, casting himself upon Christ, turn from it. When

1. Norman Grubb, *C.T. Studd* (Fort Washington: Christian Literature Crusade, 1972), 141.

a person says he is a Christian but also exhibits a cavalier attitude toward his personal sin, something is wrong.

10. Has a Vibrant Prayer Life–Simply stated, prayer is work. Yes, joys, emotions and sometimes even ecstasies, as well as sweet fellowship worshiping the Lord, are all experienced in prayer. But many believers will testify that their prayer life can become dull, arduous, and seemingly lifeless. We would hope that in our lives and in the lives of all of Christ's disciples, prayer would become a consuming desire of the heart, particularly as we fellowship with Jesus as a way of life. New believers must learn the purpose of prayer, the content of prayer, the methods of prayer, the place of prayer, the time of prayer, the motive for prayer, and the perseverance of prayer. And of course, prayer includes the crucial element of faith. Prayer is the conduit for expressing trust in our sovereign, loving Father. The new disciple has a lot to learn about prayer, but the key to a vibrant prayer life is to understand that the Christian life is a walk with Christ and the building of a relationship with Christ. The dimension of walking by faith in a growing, loving, trusting relationship (somewhat like a healthy marriage relationship between a husband and wife) is the means to maintaining a vibrant prayer life for the believer. Viewing prayer as a relationship with Christ should also take a little bit of the work out of the endeavor.

11. Shines the Light–Whether it is learning to be a verbal witness for one's Christian faith or simply the action of growing into Christ-like behavior, a young disciple of Christ exhibits growth that tells the world she is a follower of Jesus. The new believer has a life within that cannot be contained and consequently, she is the "light of the world." This radiant behavior is neither rote, dutiful, nor legalistic in its demeanor. When Christ reigns in the heart, others are sure to know. Even the quietest and shyest individual will display a steady, radiant confidence flowing from the presence of the Holy Spirit, assuring that Christ will both be seen and gain glory through her life. A Christian's words, life, actions and interactions, expressions, and responses all can serve to reflect the One who is the true "Light of the world"!

12. Integrates Faith and Life–One of the dangers that faces most every Christian is the possibility of fleeing from or living in denial regarding the issues of everyday life and existence in the "real" world. Fleeing and hiding from life as a form of world repudiation neither fulfills the

Great Commission, nor overtly expresses the glory of God to others. The call of the believer is to live out and apply her faith in every area of life. The disciple of Christ is to grow in her understanding of biblical faith and then apply what she learns to everyday life, particularly in her relationship with others.

Salt and light (Matthew 5:13-16) are metaphors that speak of influence, impact, and preservation (deterring evil in the world). As we learn of Christ and become like Christ, we reflect Christ in the world around us. Therefore, the believer will want to allow Christ to influence her academic world, leisure world, business practices, personal life, "love" life, reading or hobbies, etc. The disciple who integrates faith into life will avoid the two powerful temptations: 1) hiding in a separated shelter; and 2) squelching faith so that it only impacts religious practices.

13. Forgives Others–Over the years, as I have been involved in ministry, I have come to believe that the ability to forgive others is the most convincing trait proving that a person is a true believer in Christ. Forgiving others may be the most significant real fruit of grace and transformation flowing from a believer's heart. If a disciple of Christ truly understands the grace, patience, and mercy that God demonstrates in forgiving her as a flagrant sinner against him, then the most natural and obvious expression of that forgiveness will be the ability (as difficult as it may seem) to forgive others who have hurt her. Forgiveness by God translates into a spirit of forgiveness toward all others. The bottom line is that the growing disciple has a deep regard for God's forgiveness of her sin and in turn will learn to forgive those who injure her, no matter how painful the transgression might be. The disciple who is sensitive to her own sin and to God's forgiveness is also able to say two of the most difficult words to express in the human language. She can say, "I'm sorry." Understanding the humility of the cross makes a person both forgiving and willing to apologize.

14. Has New Attitudes/Words–The new believer often has amassed a great reservoir of sinful thoughts and practices from the past. Overcoming long held patterns of sinful thinking (and the behavior that results from them) can be very difficult. The presence of the Holy Spirit in the life of the disciple is enormous, however, and deep change is possible. God loves working in the believer's heart and changing

the inner person. The disciple has new attitudes about himself and about life. He also has new language habits. His words will change because his heart has changed. The Holy Spirit is present to work on the evils of the heart. Old attitudes, based on inherent selfishness, are slowly chiseled away by the presence of the Spirit; and new attitudes, formed by the Word of God and led by the Spirit, become ingrained in the heart. It is not unusual to see negative attitudes such as a critical and judgmental spirit, a complaining and negative spirit, jealousy, envy, covetousness, pride and arrogance, self-centeredness, anger, greed, resentment, bitterness, doubt, distrust, fear, cynicism, hostility, hatred, revenge, rebellion, apathy, self-pity, callousness, and blame-shifting being replaced by the fruit of the Spirit. The fruit of the Spirit produces a life evidenced by these attitudes: love, joy, peace, patience, kindness, goodness, faithfulness, gentleness, self-control, as well as by attitudes such as contentment, compassion and sympathy, gratitude and thankfulness, faith, hope, humility, submission, respect and cooperation, honesty, conscientiousness, courage, and confidence in God.

Moreover, what comes out of the mouth of the believer in Christ also changes, often dramatically. Words are powerful and, used wrongly, can be quite painful to others. And sadly, as Jesus states above, words demonstrate the realities of the heart. James tells his readers, "If anyone thinks he is religious and does not bridle his tongue but deceives his heart, this person's religion is worthless," (James 1:26). Words of encouragement and positive, helpful conversation should be a way of life for the disciple of Jesus. Other redeeming uses of the tongue would include praise of God in word or song, and appropriate praise and affirmation of others, words of affection and friendship, expressions of joy, humble rebuke and admonition of others, confession both of sin and of one's faith, acknowledging Christ as Lord, making oaths, vows and promises before God based on personal trustworthiness, offering words of thanksgiving and gratitude, preaching, teaching, and inspiring others for Christ.

15. Worships–Simply stated, worship is declaring God's honor, glory, praise, and worthiness. There is no one like our God! However, in the disciple's life, worship that is in spirit and in truth cannot be taken for granted. The Father seeks such worshipers (John 4:21–24). Real worship requires repentance and confession. The disciple cannot truly worship while holding on to a rebellious, disobedient attitude. The new

believer learns that worship is not a matter of simply following or accommodating to a routine or rote set of prayers and liturgy. True worship must be guided solely by the Scriptures. It is both corporate and private. It is done in reverence and awe of the living God. It involves petition, prayers, intercession, and thanksgiving. Believers worship as recipients of God's lavish grace in their lives and from a motive of gratitude. All of life is an act of worship but corporate worship in the body of Christ exalts the Lord and ministers to his servants as a body of believers. False worship occurs when a person sees himself as large and God as small. People are always prone toward false worship. True worship bows before Jesus and declares, "Worthy is the Lamb!" The disciple of Christ is one who lifts up voice, heart, and life to the triune God. This trinity of dedication is the worship that exalts the One who gave himself as a sacrifice for his people, a sacrifice that required going to the cross. A true disciple wants to worship!

16. Has a Changed Heart–The necessity for changes in the inner person have been addressed briefly above in the section on "new attitudes/ words," but the emphasis here, and one that is absolutely necessary for even mature disciples of Jesus, is to show that God is concerned about the heart. Inner realities, rather than outward behaviors, must be our focus. Outward behavior and conformity to God's law and standard can be very deceptive and lead one to an attitude of self-congratulation and self-righteousness. Introspection can be dangerous, as it looks to self and risks the possibility of looking only inward; it can become depressing. But inspection (proper introspection)–looking at the heart and our progress in order to confess, repent, and rejoice in God's grace through Christ–is fully appropriate. We must always consider the motives of our hearts. We must seek the Lord and ask his Holy Spirit to open our eyes to our needs and to expose our sin(s) so that we can become more Christ-like. We cannot permit external behavior to deceive us into thinking that everything is well within. For the new disciple, this deeper or more serious awareness may not occur at first. A young Christian may find so many new behaviors to change that she focuses only on conformity to outward expectations. An effort to please others can easily set in, one that is accomplished by "doing." But spending quiet time in the Word and in the presence of God will soon confirm the reality that she must deal both honestly and decisively with the issues of the heart. A believer must not fall

into the deception that "doing" is more important than "being." God is concerned first and foremost about the disciple's heart.

17. Is Committed to the Church–A seminary colleague once stated to me, "The church is Christ's bride, but she is one ugly bride." He was speaking of the church universal I'm sure, but I fear that we have fallen into the belief that the local church is the ugly face of Christ's bride, filled with so many warts and bumps and disfigurements that the serious Christian should have nothing to do with her. Yes, the local church is messy. It is filled with and led by sinners. It displays hypocrisy, contradictions, and shameful behavior. But Christ died for his church, and the Apostle Paul, in essence, poured out his life to start local churches, most of which exhibited numerous spiritual problems. Therefore, I would like to propose that a real disciple of Christ will become a baptized member of the local church who participates in the life of the church as a committed part of the body of Christ. No matter how the disciple comes to faith in Christ, he must transition from being an individual follower of Christ to an active member of Christ's church on a local and corporate level. The disciple should maintain a growing appreciation of the local church, despite its failings and weaknesses. And as a member of the church, the follower of Christ should be loyal to her, serve her with his gifts, abilities and financial support, and minister within the church. Attending a local church is a priority but a true follower of Christ should do much, much more. He must love the church in every way possible.

18. Grows in Assurance of Salvation–The new disciple will often have cause for alarm because of her sins and failures (and sometimes youthful stupidity). The disciple of Jesus needs reassurance or a confidence that her sins (in both number and magnitude) cannot undermine her secure relationship with the Father who has forgiven and accepts her unconditionally. Unfortunately, as believers we often doubt both God's love and the work of Christ. We look at ourselves and our sins and we allow our hearts to become crestfallen and discouraged. The disciple must understand her adoption into the family of God. Assurance comes from the finished work of Christ on the cross on behalf of the believer. God's work and his calling in the lives of his people cannot be undone. A Christian might become undone by her sin, but Christ's blood covers sins, takes away guilt and shame, and assures the believer of finished and complete pardon. In order to gain assurance,

the believer must always look to the cross, every day, even every moment. It is clear that assurance of salvation and security in Christ must be based solely on his work and that work alone. Thank God that we as Christians can rest assured that we are held in Christ's hand, in the Father's hand, and that no one can snatch us out of this powerful grasp (John 10:27–30). Jesus declared, "I and the Father are one!" And we are theirs! What assurance for the disciple of Christ!

19. Has a Biblical Worldview–A disciple must learn that a walk with Christ involves living all of life under Christ's Lordship and his Word. We have addressed this category to some extent in the two descriptions above, "Lives to Glorify God" and "Integrates Faith and Life." However, what I want to address here is the need for every disciple of Christ to recognize that she as a believer is to live every area of life to the glory of God based upon God's vocational calling in her life. God can use the disciple's vocation to effectively glorify him. "So whether you eat or drink, or whatever you do, do all to the glory of God," (1 Corinthians 10:31). A biblical world and life view means that there is no area of life over which Jesus Christ is not Lord. Therefore, the disciple of Christ does not need to be a church worker, a full-time Christian employee, a minister or a missionary in order to glorify God. The thoughtful disciple (and we hope all followers of Christ are thinking about the implications of their faith) will seek to glorify God in every area of life and take those areas of life captive for Christ her Lord–academics, dating, marriage, work, worship, living in her neighborhood, service, family life and parenthood, politics, recreation, hobbies, leisure, etc. All of life is to be lived to the glory of God and there is no area of life in which God cannot be glorified. A biblical world and life view transforms the manner in which the disciple of Christ views everything in the world and particularly her vocation. It is God's world and a Christian can serve God in all of life!

20. Exhibits Concern for Others–We might call this attribute the spirit of or for evangelism. When the Gospel takes hold in a person's life and this person truly finds Christ, real growth occurs. Such an individual begins asking some very hard questions about the people around him, those who live in his world, and whom he loves. The new believer begins to ask questions about others and his relationship with and understanding of God. He begins to wonder, "What is going to happen to that person's–my friend or family member's–soul?" "Is she going

to hell?" "Does he know Jesus?" "Is she hurting?" "How can I help?" "How can I explain the joy of this new life to him?" Sometimes the growing disciple is highly bothered by the spiritual plight of others. Most new believers are consumed with Christ, salvation, and those in need of the Gospel. They look at the multitudes and like Christ, their hearts are filled with compassion (Matthew 9:35–38), an emotion that impacts one's inner being. Such expression of feelings for others is a sure sign that Gospel assimilation has occurred in the heart of the disciple.

## Conclusion

Ultimately, disciple investing is participating in the work of making disciples, a work that Jesus has initiated and is doing in his "called ones'" lives. Christ is still calling men, women, and boys and girls to follow him, and Christ is still changing lives one person at a time. He invites us to not only follow him, but to become fishers of people. We are both fishers and disciple investors when we engage in the disciple making process *he* is doing, and those endeavors happen when we invest ourselves in the lives of others! We need to continue to hear and heed his compelling call to each of us, "Follow me, and I will make you fishers of men" (Matthew 4:19).

Please see the Appendix, in which I have provided a simple chart that I created with the help of a class of Reformed Theological Seminary students. This tool might be useful for assisting a disciple investor in evaluating the progress of a growing believer. The categories and answers listed are not infallible or comprehensive, but hopefully they are helpful for thinking through what we might call the stages of Christian growth or development. You could use it as a survey tool or simply ask the questions in conversation. The hope, of course, is to provide a basis for diagnosing a disciple's status or progress in his/her walk with Christ, and to understand needs that should be addressed.

## Questions for Reflection

1. Looking at all of the "Attributes of a Disciple" listed in this chapter, which do you think is most difficult to cultivate or exhibit in today's culture? What is the easiest?

2. If you were to prioritize the list of "Attributes of a Disciple" what would be your top five most important? Explain your rationale.

3. If possible to explain, how do you think the heart of the growing believer is best assessed?

## Action Points

1. Find a person who would be willing to take the "Christian Walk" assessment located in the Appendix and ask if they would want to discuss their answers.

2. Here is an interesting exercise: Find a time to ask your pastor or another Christian leader what they think about the "Attributes of a Disciple" list and get their opinion about what they think are the most important attributes.

# 6

# Difficulties
## Problems You Might Face

ANY TIME WE EMBRACE another person enough to be willing to invest in their faith and growth as a Christian, we are sure to confront difficulties. Working with people is not easy because we all struggle with weaknesses, failures, sins, and our fallen human nature. So, it is only honest and reasonable to address a few of the common difficulties that one might face when pouring himself into another individual on a regular basis. I am quite sure that this list could be much more extensive, but I am limiting my focus to just a few of the difficulties that I have experienced over the years.

## Potential People Problems

Once we decide and commit to become involved in and intertwined with another person's life, we will soon realize that this endeavor, although filled with great potential for blessing, inevitably includes some real personal or interpersonal challenges and hurdles. People (including ourselves, of course) have problems and those problems inevitably will surface in the course of a long-term relationship. In the Evangelism course that I teach at RTS Charlotte, I always tell the students, during the lecture on motivation, that one of the reasons that we fail to evangelize is because we don't want to get entangled in other people's pain: people's (and especially new believers') lives are messy. We don't want to deal with the mess or the pain. I also often tell our students–and it is true for anyone who wants to engage in others' lives in any real and helpful manner–that being a pastor is similar to the life of a once-famous 1950s television character by the name of Ed Norton. Ed Norton, played by the exceptionally gifted actor Art Carney, was the close friend and fellow tenant dweller (along with their wives, Trixie and Alice) of Ralph Kramden. Ralph was played by the incomparable, high profile actor of his era, Jackie Gleason. The television series was based on the lives of New York City blue collar workers and was called "The Honeymooners." Ralph Kramden's occupation was as a bus driver for the fictional Gotham Bus Company, while Norton's job was as a New York City *sewer worker*. Yes, I turn to these often young (and maybe idealistic) students, aspiring to be potential pastors and full-time Christian workers, and encourage them by telling them that they are heading into a profession that is similar to working in the New York sewer system. Now, honestly, the ministry isn't quite that bad, but I simply want to remind them that when they become deeply and seriously involved in other people's lives, they will discover that they are going to get their "spiritual" hands very dirty and soiled by what they see, do, and experience. This reality is also true, at least at times, for anyone who wants to do disciple investing. If that includes you, be prepared: you will see some ugly, smelly stuff first hand when you are committed to going the distance with the other person, rain or shine!

## Resistance

Resistance is a frequent response to serious spiritual pursuits. When meeting with a resistant person (or a resistant stage in the process), the key to continuing the relationship, assuming that the relational door is still open, will be derived by your love and your foundation of trust. If you have developed even the minutest level of trust in the relationship, resistance has potential to break down. Ensuing openness can occur. If we are honest with ourselves, we cannot blame unbelievers, new believers, or others once involved with the local church, for being skittish about meeting with or listening to someone who represents a gospel organization or ministry. The disciple investor must prayerfully entrust himself to the Lord for a providential softening of the resistant heart with hopes for a welcome response to spiritual overtures. The goal of any encounter with *anyone* is to love that person with the love of God, without an expectation of a desired response and regardless of how he responds. Sincerity is the beginning of building a trust relationship, and real trust is the only way the relationship is going to go forward in a profitable and positive manner. Resistance is overcome by love, trust, and lots of prayer.

## Inconsistency

Life is very unpredictable and that is often true of people as well. If there is one consistent truism about people and their behavior, it is that people are not consistent in their behavior. This is especially true when another person is speaking into an individual's life, meeting regularly with him and holding him accountable (even if the accountability is loosely structured). The main point to note in this regard is that when working with another person in a disciple investing situation, the disciple investor needs to recognize, on the front end, that the other person will not always respond to communications on time, will not always show up to meet, will not always explain why he did not do either of the above, and will frequently appear to disregard counsel or advice that you have given him. People's inconsistent behaviors make living or working with them very difficult. But such is the life of working with others in any type of ministry or relationship setting. Patience, as mentioned above, is a necessary attitude, while perseverance is a wonderful attribute to display toward those who don't seem to be cooperating with your schedules, design, and plans. At some point, however, you as the disciple investor will have to make a decision among three possible options:

1. Decide if the person is making enough encouraging progress such that you will continue to meet with him in spite of his inconsistencies.

2. Decide if you must confront the person with specific examples of inconsistency, garner a response from him, and discern whether or not he truly wants to take the disciple investing relationship seriously enough to change, allowing you both to continue moving forward in the relationship.

3. Decide if the person is simply wasting your time and energy, thus necessitating a change of relationship with him, a change that might lead you to focus upon someone else.

None of the above decisions can be termed "bad ones," as each requires making wise (although possibly painful) determinations on behalf of the disciple investor. You know yourself, your life demands and responsibilities, and your schedule. In my opinion, the disciple investor should expect some inconsistency from all but the most structured and conscientious participants. I lean toward options 1 and 2. In the long run, you will probably see continued progress in the other person's life, as well as a sense of gratitude on both of your parts, as you look back at what God has done over time.

## Lack of Commitment

This problem is actually much more serious than the dilemma of inconsistency. Inconsistency usually derives from some failure or weakness on the part of the disciple and potentially can be improved upon or shorn up with some corrective effort or forthright communication. Lack of commitment, however, is often a matter of one's will and displays a deep failure in desire and motivation. If the other person really doesn't want to show up in order to discuss spiritual matters, she won't. If she doesn't value the priority for spiritual growth, there are bigger heart issues. There is nothing more frustrating than to have one person strongly impassioned for a cause and the other person lacking any passion. Put the two together and fireworks will occur–but only on your part! I believe that there are only two solutions for motivating a person with a lack of commitment, and both are related to the Lord's work:

1) The person must be awakened spiritually by the Holy Spirit–all you can do is pray until that awakening occurs; 2) The Lord may bring a crisis in the individual's life that makes her see her absolute dependence, as well as her brevity in this life, thus motivating her to respond to spiritual opportunities that present themselves in her life. It is possible that the disciple investor will have to drop the uncommitted person from his disciple investing intentions until she becomes truly committed to growing in the Lord.

## Failed Agendas

In the disciple investing process, you as the disciple investor, will attempt to get to know the other person well enough to be able to minister to him in a fruitful and helpful way, possibly even in a directed way. As you spend time with anyone with whom you want to invest, eventually (and sometimes immediately) you will discern areas of need in his life that would be well addressed by Scripture. At least you hope for such an opportunity. In this process of discernment, you may determine certain topics of either interest or need that provide a sense of direction for your conversation. Always, you want to get to know the other person, while building a real and natural relationship with him, and not forcing topics or subjects upon your times meeting together. Many times, when working with both students on campus and adults in the church, I would think ahead of time and give thoughtful consideration to what our time together might look like. Possibly, we might need to talk about a given temptation, a specific conflict, a certain sin, a struggling relationship, leadership and vision, their job or studies, and the list could go on. It is only reasonable for the disciple investor, if he is going to take the time and effort (often sacrificially) to meet with another person, to plan ahead and determine how some of the time together should be used. Proper stewardship of his and the other person's time is at stake. Depending on the depth and security of the relationship, I recommend telling the other person, "Hey, let's get together and discuss _____ question or situation. What do you think? When can we meet?" However, I discovered quite a few times that I had to be flexible in *my* goals and purposes for the meeting (note: I am a severe planner and don't like flexing too much if possible). The other person might disclose a new avenue of trouble or a recent question that has arisen in his life. Therefore, my *agenda* would have to wait. My planned session would "fail." Over the years, I discovered that the Lord used many of these spontaneous (or "failed agenda") conversations in his timing, so that ultimately, they were not failed at all. But they did feel like a failure at the time. Thankfully, I could flex and find him working his plan in it all, after all!

## Questions for Reflection

1. What type of personal problems (others' problems) might concern you as you consider getting involved in a disciple investing relationship?

2. How do you think the Lord will help you as you deal with a disciple's problems?

3. Which do you think is more difficult to work with: 1) a resistant person; 2) an inconsistent person; or 3) an uncommitted person? Why do you feel this way?

4. How do you feel about "dropping" a person who has become unresponsive in the disciple investing process? How should you go about dropping him and moving on?

## Action Points

1. Do some research in order to find a book, article, or video that might help you better understand the struggles of other people (e.g., doubt, depression, anxiety, anger, resentment, bitterness, pain, lust, etc.)

2. Ask your pastoral staff about the type of materials they use to provide biblical counsel for your church.

# 7

# Diagnosis and The Role of Counseling
## Understanding the Role of the Individual

I MENTIONED EARLIER THAT I love baseball and have since I was eight years old. I'm over sixty years of age now but still very much love to play "America's pastime." I played all the way through high school and had the opportunity to walk-on to a very good team in college. I don't have any idea how that might have turned out because at that time, as described in the introduction, I became a Christian; instead of walking on, I walked away. Nevertheless, I've played baseball (and its sickly cousin, softball) off and on all my life. I enjoy fielding–shagging fly balls–more than anything else, that is if I can ever find someone to hit them to me.

However, since finding fly ball hitters is so difficult, and because I do like to throw almost as much as field, some years ago I created a pitcher's mound in my backyard. I had thrown against the wall of my house for quite some time but eventually sculptured a pitcher's mound sixty feet six inches (the major league distance) from the wall of my house. I then created a standard strike zone on the brick wall using blue painter's masking tape. I have set up (or down) a home plate at the base of the wall so that, when I feel like getting outside and exercising a bit, I can just grab a glove and a hard, rubber, dimpled batting cage baseball and step outside and throw (or pitch). I enjoy doing it enough that I could do it every day if the weather permits. However, despite the ease of going out and throwing a baseball against the wall, I much more enjoy throwing with another person. By myself, I can pitch or throw against the wall, but I miss out on the joy of catching (although on the rebound, when not errant, the ball usually returns to me in some fashion). There is nothing that can replace the pleasure of pitching and catching with another person. I probably could do that all day long (I have what is called a "rubber" arm).

However, when I was doing campus ministry with Reformed University Fellowship at the University of Florida, our leader and the founder of RUF, the Reverend Mr. Mark Lowrey, constantly reminded the staff and ministers that when it came to ministry, catching was as important (or possibly even more important) than pitching. That is, asking questions or throwing them another person's way and hearing their answers is more important than simply presenting your informative "sales" pitch! The obvious conclusion and ministry implication was, "How can you give the answers when you don't know the questions?" "How can you present your message without hearing from the other individual first?"

I'm quite sure that the concept of pitching (asking questions first) and catching (hearing out the other person) was espoused as a reaction (and an appropriate one) to the frequently used "canned" methods of evangelism that were so affluent in the 1960s and 1970s. The stereotypical method of outreach in evangelical circles during those decades was to aggressively approach a stranger, assume that he was most probably not a believer and then present as much information as possible about your beliefs, cramming the presentation into the time frame you were allowed. The thinking of the day was, "We have the answers and if you will simply listen to us for the next ten minutes (or the next hour), we can tell you what you need to know about God."

Looking back, I must say that I saw God sovereignly bless many of those encounters, as assertive and one-way directed as they may have been. Nevertheless, I believe that Mark Lowrey is right: people interested in evangelism, as well as in being disciple investors, must be "people focused" and should guide their ministry methods by an approach to ministry that is committed to discovering and responding to the needs of other people. "Pitching and catching" is simply a helpful metaphor for viewing ministry as a process of spiritual diagnosis leading to spiritual counsel and guidance based upon the Scriptures. I believe much fruitful ministry arises out of the context of pitching and catching. Why is this?

As the disciple investor begins to become involved in the lives of others and seeks to minister to them, it becomes apparent that usually the real needs of the aspiring disciple are below the surface. People don't readily admit to or express their spiritual needs (certainly not initially). Yet the reality is that the needs exist and must be addressed. Therefore, the disciple investor must learn how to ask questions of the soul. The Scriptures clearly tell us that, "The heart is deceitful above all things, and desperately sick; who can understand it? 10 'I the Lord search the heart and test the mind, to give every man according to his ways, according to the fruit of his deeds'" (Jeremiah 17:9–10).

Being a soul searcher requires that the disciple investor must make inquiries into the disciple's soul and spiritual well-being. People often resist this because it exposes their weaknesses, bad habits, poor life patterns, and deep-seeded sins. All of us would readily admit that we naturally are not drawn to exposing our deepest failings and thoughts to another individual. The process is guaranteed to involve pain and embarrassment. But I must state wholeheartedly that some of the most pleasurable aspects of my disciple investing ministry have involved the opportunity to build a trusting relationship, create an encounter consisting of mutual dialogue, and gain a platform for respectful inquiry and sharing of hearts and lives. All of this comes to pass through the art of asking genuine questions of the other individual (probing) and hearing him out without judgment or an attitude of surprise.

Disciple investors need to understand how to diagnose other individuals that the Lord brings their way. Diagnosis is a challenge in western culture, particularly in America, because of the presence of what is known as "cultural Christianity," i.e., the reality that Americans embrace some very broad definitions of what it means to be a follower of Christ. During the first decade of the twenty-first century, *Leadership Journal* unveiled the results of a national survey called "5 Kinds of Christians." The report was produced by Helen Lee and was intended to help readers understand the disparity of those who call themselves Christians in America.

I found that the most helpful insight flowing out of this survey involved the categorization of American believers. In reality, I think that the church through the ages has always encompassed these or very similar categories. These broad categories of defining a Christian make it difficult for someone interested in the personal development of another individual to determine whether or not that individual is truly a believer in the born-again or converted sense.

Here are the "5 Kinds of Christians" that the survey surfaced along with descriptors of each:[1]

1: Active Christians (19 percent)

- Believe salvation comes through Jesus Christ
- Are committed churchgoers
- Are Bible-readers
- Accept leadership positions
- Invest in personal faith development through the church
- Feel obligated to share faith; 79 percent do so

2: Professing Christians (20 percent)

- Believe salvation comes through Jesus Christ
- Focus on personal relationship with God and Jesus
- Have similar beliefs to active Christians, but different actions
- Are less involved in church, both attending and serving
- Have less commitment to Bible reading or sharing faith

3: Private Christians (24 percent)

- Comprise the largest and youngest segment
- Believe in God and doing good things
- Own a Bible, but don't read it
- Display spiritual interest, but not within church context
- Only about a third attend church at all
- Almost none are church leaders

4: Liturgical Christians (16 percent)

- Are predominantly Catholic and Lutheran
- Attend church regularly
- Show a high level of spiritual activity, mostly expressed by serving in church and/or community
- Recognize authority of the church

1. See Helen Lee, "5 Kinds of Christians" in *Leadership Journal* (October 1, 2007).

5: Cultural Christians (21 percent)

- Display little outward religious behavior or attitudes
- Are aware of God, but have little personal involvement with God
- Do not view Jesus as essential to salvation
- Affirm many ways to God
- Favor universality theology

What can one learn from the results of the *Leadership* survey? One can readily see that when an individual (particularly an American, although I think these results would be potentially true wherever there is a Christian presence) professes that he/she is a "Christian" or a "Christian believer," that person could be defining his/her faith by any of the above definitions. It is very possible that anyone who professes to be a believer might not be "born again," truly converted, a true follower of Jesus, or in a relationship with, or a lover and worshiper of the one, true, living God. Once a person professes to be a Christian, that profession of faith needs to be probed a little more deeply. What does the person mean by the label "Christian"? What does she really believe about the character of God and the person and work of Christ? Who is she truly trusting for salvation? Does she even believe in the need for personal salvation? Does she understand that being a Christian means having a personal relationship with God? What does she understand about the cross? Does she believe that she is a sinner? Does she think that good works will get her to heaven? Does she think that others need Christ in their lives or for salvation? What does she believe about faith and grace? What does she grasp about the relationship of obedience and faith?

All of these questions display the opportunistic role of "spiritual diagnosis" or "soul searching" on behalf of the disciple investor. What can one gain by asking probing questions of another person's soul? The inquisitive disciple investor can gain everything if the person is receptive, can trust the disciple investor, and is willing to be honest and forthright about inner realities and beliefs. The conviction of the one who practices the art of spiritual diagnosis is that the conversation and the dialogue is the key to real and effective ministry in another person's life.

Spiritual diagnosis is effective if the science becomes an art. The art, however, must precede the science. The science of asking questions begins by knowing the right questions to ask: in this case, questions that lend themselves to personal, spiritual insight. Below is a list of possible questions that a disciple investor uses naturally (that's the art dimension) with a disciple.

## DIAGNOSTICS: ANALYZING THE INDIVIDUAL

*(Note: Some of these categories are derived from the RUF Staff Training notebook)*

### Personal Interest: Who are You?

The starting point of spiritual diagnosis is a simple and obvious one–the potential disciple investor wants to sincerely get to know basic, introductory facts about the disciple. Almost everyone asks these types of questions as a starting point in normal social settings in which people are getting to know each other. Here are some of the essential and basic categories for getting to know others.

### Personal Information, Upbringing, Background, Etc.

Who are they? What are they like? How do they interact and relate? What characteristics stand out about them? Are there any obvious personality traits or concerns (this may come later)? Where are they from; what is their city (cities) of origin?

### Personal and Relational Background: Family, Friends, Friendships, and Love

This conversation begins with asking for information about family background. What is their family background? Did they grow up in an intact, divided, or blended family environment? What are their parents like? Are they close or disconnected with their family members, particularly their parents? What is their present relationship with both of their parents (or step-parents)? What about their siblings–do they have any? Are there any step-siblings, and what is their relationship to them? Do they have a circle of friends or any close friends? Are they looking for friendships?

## Education, Study/Major, and Work

What type and level of schooling have they accomplished? What type of schools did they attend growing up: public, private, Christian, parochial? What was their field of study? Did they enjoy their field of study? What type of job do they have now? Do they enjoy their job? Do they have any problems on the job? (This is where real ministry and the application of biblical salve occurs.)

## Interests and Avoidance

What might be some of their hobbies, interests, etc.? What do they enjoy and enjoy doing? What would be appealing to them in such a way that they would want to be involved in your church or ministry? What about your church, group, or ministry would be a "turn off" to them?

## Strengths and Weaknesses

What are their personal strong points and gifts? What stands out about them and makes them unique? What do they think their strengths might be? Are they realistic about themselves? What are some of their weaknesses and possible failings? (These are often easier to spot than potential strengths.)

## Struggles or Problems

With what are they presently struggling? Are there some obvious problems? Are there apparent behavioral, personal, mental, intellectual, or emotional problems?

## Spiritual Interest: What Do You Think about God?

For me, the most exciting realm of disciple investing and spiritual diagnosis is discovering what *any* person believes about the one, true and living God of the universe, the One who has revealed himself in the Scriptures. Once we have gotten to know some personal information about the individual, built something of a trustworthy and genuine relationship (this takes time and doesn't necessarily happen initially), the art of spiritual diagnosis involves moving the conversation into the spiritual realm. Now the fun begins! What is really true about them? What do they know about God, the Bible, and Christian faith? Is their understanding superficial or simplistic, or have they given substantial thought to what they believe? What do they say they believe and what do they really believe? Is belief personal and is it consistent with demonstrated love (passion) and conduct? What are their idols? We ask such questions knowing that we all have personal idols, loves so deep that we place them first in our lives and we cannot part with them.

Below are some categories and questions (the science) to assist a disciple investor (and an evangelist) in the spiritual diagnostic process. Now you are learning to become a physician of the soul, a blessed profession indeed!

A. Church or Religious Background Inquiry–Have they ever been involved in a church? Are they involved in a church presently? What type of church is it? Do they understand the beliefs of their church/denomination and do they agree with those beliefs? What is their view of Christians? What do they think of the local church or their past/present experience in the local church?

B. Reception or Resistance toward the Gospel–Often, during times of initial visits or appointments with potential disciples, the disciple investor will readily discern interest in the gospel and matters of faith or, conversely, will quickly perceive distrust, skepticism or rejection of both the gospel and the messenger's efforts. Frequently, the encounters involving rejection will end in a termination of the relationship and a lack of further pursuit of any viable meetings. As genuine and sincere as the disciple investor might be, such reactions are not surprising.

C. Understanding the Message of the Gospel–Do they understand the gospel? What do they think or understand about God? Who is God? What is God like–how would they define or explain God? What do they believe about the nature of man? How do they define or view sin? How do they view the cross, especially in light of their own sins? Who is Jesus? Is he divine? Was he a real human being? Why must he be both God and man? Why did he go to the cross? What about the resurrection? Why is it important? Where is Jesus now and what is he doing? How are sins forgiven? How does the believer attain the perfection that God requires? Why is Christ's life important? Why is Christ's blood important? What is the relationship of faith and works in salvation? (This is a *huge* clarification question.) What is "grace"? What is repentance? How do faith and repentance relate to conversion? What does it mean to trust, receive, commit one's life to, pray to, receive, turn to, or cast oneself upon Christ?

D. Level of, or Progress in, Christian Growth–Are they using the "means of grace," i.e., Word, prayer, worship, sacraments, fellowship, accountability? How does a Christian grow? What prevents Christian growth?

1. The Word–What is the disciple's relationship to the Scriptures? Has he ever attempted to read through any of the Bible, the entire Bible, or either the Old or New Testament? What has he read from the Bible?

2. Prayer–What is the disciple's view, understanding, and practice of prayer? What is his primary struggle with having a prayer life? Does he understand the basic elements (ACTS: Adoration, Confession, Thanksgiving, Supplication) of a vibrant prayer life?

3. Worship–Does the disciple understand the priority of worshiping with God's people, particularly in the local church? Does she understand the difference between corporate worship among God's people in the local church as opposed to worship in a parachurch setting? Does she understand the difference between God-centered worship and man-centered worship? Does she understand the role of personal worship and personal devotions?

4. Community–Does the believer value both the local church and the importance of being in fellowship with other believers of like mind? How does he view personal accountability and confession of sin? Does he see the need for personal spiritual support in his walk with the Lord? Does he value the ministry of a pastor/shepherd in his life?

5. Accountability to Christ's Body (Discipline/Oversight)–One aspect of being a part of Christ's church and in the fellowship of the church involves personal responsibility and accountability. Some helpful questions for the disciple investor to ask: What is happening in your walk with the Lord? Are you finding consistency with your use of the means of grace? With what issues in your life or with what sins are you struggling? What is your

relationship with the local church? Are there any issues between you and another/other believer/believers? Do you desire to create a means of personal accountability for your walk with the Lord in regard to challenging areas in your life such as sexuality, time and money management, Christian fellowship, etc.? Do you have or need a means to assist you with more structure/discipline in your life?

6. Character (Fruit of the Spirit; Heart change)–Character is difficult to appraise; it is not readily apparent because, ironically, people can be good liars. We are all able to put on false fronts and positive outward appearances and cover up our true feelings. However, when the Holy Spirit is working in a person's life, the person usually acknowledges various heart changes that are occurring. His changing character is exciting to him and often becomes obvious to the close onlooker. He also willingly reveals what is happening in his heart and life. All of the fruits listed in the "fruit of the Spirit" passage in Galatians, and character traits such as integrity, conviction of sin, conscientiousness, perseverance, dedication, unselfishness, sacrificial living, honoring others first, forgiving others, generosity, etc., begin to develop and surface.

   Some questions to ask the individual would be: How do you see yourself changing? How do you feel about your sin? What are you experiencing in your relationships to others? What would you say are the positive changes going on in your life and heart? How does being a Christian affect your life at home, in marriage and at the work place (or school)? Have you experienced any "eye opening" changes in understanding yourself? Are there areas in your life that feel inconsistent with your heart and belief?

7. Hopes and Dreams–Questions to ask the individual would include: What do you hope to accomplish in life (or in your remaining years, as the Lord wills)? What are the deepest desires you would like to have fulfilled? What is your vision for your life, or your family, or your career? Have you given your hopes over to the Lord and his lordship in your life? Can you live contentedly if the Lord diverts or changes your plans?

## The Need for Diagnosis

What are the purposes of spiritual diagnosis? What can be accomplished through the process of soul inspection? The benefit of this particular disciple investing ministry lies in its strength of dealing with the inner realities of people's lives and thoughts and helping them to be open and transparent with their problems and struggles. As difficult as it might be to gain another person's trust and to hear her share deep and sometimes dark realities, the profits of such a ministry are immensurable. The reality is that the disciple investor must take the initiative in the life of another in order to discover the spiritual problems that most certainly exist there. With God's help, the disciple investor must begin with inquiry (questioning), then deepen the probing through further questions and if possible, become like a surgeon of the soul, discovering the areas needing repair through the salve or medicine of applied Scripture. Every person experiences personal struggles, relational hurts, heart problems, and secret sins and temptations that assail the soul and make living life–and the Christian life–challenging and difficult. Diagnosis intends to bring such problems to the surface in order to address them. Asking genuine questions with a sincere love and respect for others ought to be a cardinal quality of any believer's life and ministry.

## The Purposes of Spiritual Diagnosis

Here are some specific purposes of spiritual diagnosis:

1. The Revelation of Concealed or False Spirituality: Removing the Mask
   People are experts in covering up their sins, needs, and problems. They are gifted at putting on false fronts. So, we must discover the answer to this question: "Are you truly interested in spiritual things or are you putting up a front?"

2. Poor Theological Understanding: Unveiling Poor Thinking
   I have discovered that many people in and around the church do not fully understand the work of Christ on the cross. Therefore, they live day to day without assurance of salvation, without confidence that God loves them and accepts them through Christ, and without full peace of mind in regard to their eternal destiny. These believers do not really understand what salvation means or is. The disciple investor will never err in making the effort to take an evangelistic approach to

a first encounter with another person, including a professed believer. When the subject of spiritual interest (or religion, or faith) comes up, it is not inappropriate to pursue the person's understanding of the cross and the work of Christ on behalf of the believer. Has this person trusted Christ for her salvation? What does this trust mean to her? How has she responded to this act of faith?

3. Verbalization of Understanding: Explaining Beliefs as Able

This diagnostic purpose is simple and straightforward. It is also very telling and revealing. If the disciple investor receives honest answers (weak answers are also very telling), she can shed a vast amount of gospel light on the matters and questions at hand. This form of diagnosis requires basic questioning in the realm of explanation. It attempts to expose weaknesses in understanding. Whatever the topic, simply ask disciples to try to explain their understanding or position. Whenever disciples are unclear or make apparent wrong statements, ask them to clarify or explain their understanding once more. Some sample questions might be: "How would you explain what a Christian is?" "How does a person go about becoming a Christian?" "What is God like?" "Why did Jesus have to die?" "What happens to people when they die?" "Why is Jesus or Christianity unique?" "Do you have any problems with the Bible?"

4. Deep Hurts Exposed: Finding Out What Wounds They Carry

Time and trust are involved at this stage of diagnosis and this stage often doesn't begin at the initiation of the relationship. However, some people have no one they trust to whom they can tell their secrets, so occasionally, they will expose revelations of the soul in a surprisingly fast manner. When they expose their wounds and baggage, the diagnosis isn't necessarily over and the disciple investor may have to ask them to give more details in order to comprehend the depth of the pain. No matter what, however, when they open their lives and hearts to a more mature listener, a tremendous level of trust (or potential for trust) has occurred.

The most basic and direct question to ask at this stage is, "Are you interested in hearing what God (the Bible or God's Word) says about that problem or situation?" In asking this question, the disciple investor will readily discover the level of resistance to God, his Word, his "expertise," and the necessity for real personal change. Hopefully people will answer in the affirmative. Not only do they need to hear truth (God's Word), but the reality is that they need a relational context to be healed as well. They need the disciple investor's love and input. Ultimately, I would suggest that the wounded need the community or the body of Christ to help them through the healing process.

5. Real Relationships Realized: Discovering Who Really Cares For and Loves Them

Certainly this is a question or issue that is difficult to uncover unless there is an obvious strained relationship between the person and members of her family. Of course, people will often shift the focus to family members or parents if the subject of personal pain arises and the sources of that pain are discussed. The real goal of such a conversation, however, is not to point blame at others who contributed to the pain or to pry into the person's family secrets or private personal life, but to discover if the person is devoid of a sense of being loved and/or does feel loved by someone. Some questions to consider: Who among the disciple's family members cares about her? Who are her close friends and confidants and who can she trust to be by her side in tough times? Who is truly loyal to her? Does she feel loved by anyone?

## Applying Biblically Based Answers

As we consider the role of Scripture and truth as a ministry in another's life, we commit ourselves to the reality that, through the power of the Holy Spirit, the Word of God is powerfully able to transform the hearts and lives of both ourselves and others. Where do we turn to find the answers to our struggles, problems, and painful experiences? The answer that comforts, encourages, and heals is none other than the very Word of God. The necessary ministry of diagnosis is only useful if the disciple investor understands the ministry of scriptural application to the soul's open wounds, so you do need to do some homework or study. The sources of these wounds manifest themselves in the following *three* areas or domains of life. Look carefully for potential problems; we all have them:

1. Knowledge and Understanding—We want to discover what people know and believe on the more basic level. The disciple investor must recognize that spiritual and biblical illiteracy and ignorance is vast in

our culture. And this lack of knowledge is growing steadily, right before our eyes. The Scriptures are powerful and grasping them means that the disciple investor holds a sword in his hand, heart, and head. The topics of knowledge to cover are simple. Based upon categories of what is traditionally termed "systematic theology," the big categories of knowledge to be covered would include:

A. God

- Who is he? What is he like?

- Can we know him and how is that possible?

- What is the Trinity (in the simplest of terms) and why does the Trinity matter?

- What does it mean that he is a creator?

B. Scripture

- Why is the Bible important?

- What is the primary message of the Bible?

- How is the Bible trustworthy? (Inspired/Infallible/Without error)

C. Man

- Creation and the Image of God

- Sin, sin nature, sin's power and penalty, and man's inability to please God or save himself

D. Christ

- Who is he?
  1. God/Deity
  2. Man/Humanity

- What did he do?
  1. His life, suffering, and death on the cross
  2. His resurrection, ascension, and being seated at God's right hand
  3. His coming as the judge of the world

E. Salvation

- Why is the cross important for forgiveness?

- How does a person become a Christian?

- What are repentance and faith?

- How does a person/sinner get right with God? (Justification)

- How do we grow as Christians? (Sanctification)

- How does the Holy Spirit help us live the Christian life?

F. The Church

- Why is the church important?

- What are the "means of grace"?

- How should we worship?

- What are the sacraments and why are they important?

- What is Christian community?

G. The End of the World

- What is the nature of death, judgment, heaven and hell?

- What about the second coming of Christ?

- What will we be like in heaven? (Glorification)

2. Attitudes, Loves, and Passions–Notice the often obvious presence of negative emotions or attitudes: complaints, a critical spirit, harshness, obvious self-life and ego, non-receptivity (toward the disciple investor and his ministry), anger, cynicism, doubt, pessimism, worry, angst, fear, hurt, and distrust. At the same time, positive emotions can exist that can be quite encouraging: cheerfulness and joy, gratitude, contentedness, a servant spirit, patience, a caring outlook toward others. It is important to note that people can be overwhelmed particularly by "bad" heart attitudes and therefore become discouraged about the future. The disciple investor's presence and listening ear alone can be powerful. The disciple investor must also discern what the individual is tempted to place first in his life. What does he love first and foremost? What are his idols? What is his primary focus or the center of attention at the present time? What drives or motivates him more than anything else in life?

3. Practices: Observation of behavior–One of the disciple investor's goals in spending time with those in whom he is investing is to discover

what people are doing with their time and their schedules. How do they go about making decisions and what kind of decisions are they making? Upon what basis are they making these decisions? What types of relationships are in their world and what types of activities are they involved in on a regular basis? What are their daily or weekly lives like? Are they using or pursuing the means of grace? Are they lazy time wasters? Are their lives filled with pornography or other potentially deep-seeded sins and addictive habits (technology infinitum)? How are they interacting with the body of Christ? What is their relationship to the local church? How far away from the local church are they? We should also discern if the believer can relate to other believers of the same or opposite sex. Have these individuals developed or are they missing necessary interpersonal/social skills? Christian groups have the potential to draw the socially inept/lonely.

## Methods of Spiritual Diagnosis

1. The Use of Questions–As mentioned above, questions are the key to diagnosis. Not just using a few questions, but often asking question after question is a necessary approach in order to get to the core of the problems and issues existing in a person's life and soul.

   Asking questions as a ministry requires the following:

   A. Digging Deeper–Questions lead to questions. In the course of conversation in a disciple investing context, asking only one question is usually not enough. One question allows for a superficial answer. There is a need for asking many questions. Your ministry is one of questioning. The reason a disciple investor needs to listen and be patient is because ministry requires multiple questions that probe deeper and deeper beyond both the original question and the initial answer. Questions lead to answers but answers should naturally lead to more questions. As a matter of fact, the artful question asker will learn discipline in the number of questions used or proposed.

   B. Probing vs. Radical Surgery–Probing, through the use of asking questions, is absolutely necessary if the disciple investor is going to engage with the heart realities of the individual. But

74

sometimes gentle probing is not enough. The disciple investor should never set out or intend to violate the soul of another believer, as needy as the person might be. Questions, revelations, and conversation ought to be mutually respectful and voluntary. However, there are times when "radical surgery" is required. If the person is dealing with or hiding a deep problem or sin that has imminent negative consequences, or is simply too ugly or gruesome for anyone to live with happily, then confrontation (or radical surgery) may be required.

2. Listening for/to Verbal Cues–People will tell a disciple investor a lot about themselves, their beliefs, their concerns, and their passions if she simply listens closely to their words. What might not be immediately apparent while they are speaking nevertheless may reveal some covert misunderstanding if the disciple investor attempts to clarify the vague and unclear statements being espoused.

3. Biblical Analysis–Foundational to all spiritual or soul diagnosis is the inherent assumption that the disciple investor has at least an adequate, working knowledge of Scripture (see "Biblical Understanding," as addressed in Chapter 1). Failure to know the Scriptures presupposes the failure of ministry in the life and soul of another believer. Of course, as mentioned earlier, having adequate knowledge does not require a seminary education (as helpful as that might be, depending upon the seminary). However, extra study of the Bible is a necessity, as is an ability to apply the Bible's teachings with some spiritual common sense. The combination of your own personal Christian experience, supported with at least some minor people skills and a little life wisdom, is inestimable in its value for soul care and searching. The effective soul searcher understands that the Bible does have the answer for the soul's deepest problems and will attempt to research the appropriate scriptural answer to apply to an expressed or diagnosed spiritual need.

4. Continued Analysis–Reading Between the Lines: People will answer your questions but sometimes they divulge little helpful information. Real heart-focused ministry keeps asking questions. The simplest perceptive question that can continue to move the conversation along and clarify uncertain statements is, "What do you mean by that comment?" Other useful questions would be, "Could you tell me more?" "Could you clarify that statement?" Try to avoid taking their answers

for granted or assuming that what they said is accurate or complete no matter how direct or plainspoken they may be. Usually, the disciple investor must listen carefully for potential inferences about a person's private or secret life. The individual who is naturally perceptive, insightful and intuitive will sense the quiet overtures from others as he takes a glimpse into their lives.

5. Looking for the Bottom Line–What is Actually Happening? Swapping stories and engaging in ministry conversation is never the final goal of the "soul searching" disciple investor. Although the verbal sharing of lives is an obvious sign of Christian fellowship and mutual friendship, it also serves the purpose of discovering what is actually going on in an individual's heart. All of the surface conversations, as pleasurable as they might be, are intended by the disciple investor to assist in ministering to the other person's real (and possibly deepest) needs. Asking questions, listening for verbal cues, and analyzing answers biblically are ultimately avenues for discovering spiritual needs and providing the appropriate biblical answers. We want to know answers to these questions: What are their true "spiritual" struggles? What are the sins with which they are dealing? How can we help them in their walks with Christ?

## Revelations of Diagnosis

When the disciple investor engages in the diagnostic process, many issues of the soul will inevitably surface. Here are some thoughts about the most common revelations derived from spiritual diagnosis:

1. Spiritual Perceptions

   A. The Relationship Between Faith and Works–As previously discussed, I believe that over 50 percent of the people in the "pew" (local church) struggle with assurance of salvation. Something that often clouds this crucial issue is the *problem* of false assurance of salvation: people may believe they are saved when they are not, or that their salvation permits simultaneous involvement in "Christian license" (living in sin).

   B. Their View of Sin–Is Sin Personal and Real? The subject of sin is often an uncomfortable one. People do not want to admit that they are sinners since such an admission would appear to confirm that they are bad people. But if confessing one's own sinfulness is one of the critical steps toward repenting and becoming a believer in Christ, then the nature of personal sin needs to be confronted. Sin–disobedience, failure, and shame–must be a topic of conversation in the disciple investing relationship. Some people will be desirous of confessing a specific sin with another person due to the relief of conscience such an admission might bring. Others will avoid their guilt and shame initially, at least until they recognize that sin is their biggest problem in the Christian life, and that they must confess, repent of, and forsake personal sin.

2. Need for Guidance and Counsel

A. Fear and Worry–One of the most natural areas of counsel and life guidance that a disciple investor faces is another person's fear and worries, particularly as related to the future. Ultimately, the disciple investor encourages individuals with the assurance that God will guide and take care of them as they move forward in faith.

B. Pain/Bitterness–Bad experiences from one's past can grow like a cancer and create memories and distrust like none other. Nothing touches so many people so deeply as a painful life experience, particularly an early life experience. Followers of Christ need direct counseling in these very personal areas of the soul. New believers are ready and eager to follow the Lord and can grow spiritually at what appear to be exponential rates. However, the bitterness of a nagging memory can disrupt such growth. Bitterness (along with complaining) is a sin that robs people of both the joy of the Holy Spirit and the assurance of God's presence. Two particular doctrines that one must address in order to deal with pain and bitterness are 1) the sovereignty of God; and 2) the grace (and strength) of God.

C. Resentment/Anger–Closely related to pain and bitterness are the spiritual weeds of the heart known as resentment and anger. As a matter of fact, both of these heart attitudes, if left unchecked, can lead to the cancer of bitterness and ultimately will destroy the soul.

D. Providing Answers

1. Looking for Solutions–When faced with problems of the soul, our western culture seems to look everywhere but in a God-focused direction (special revelation, i.e., the Bible). We see more "self-help" books and materials in Christian bookstores than one can imagine. We listen to various "Christian" leaders and televangelists who espouse some sort of positive (or "possibility") thinking that uses the Bible as a promise-pill method. Yet these methods are completely devoid of an honest assessment of personal sin or a frank portrayal of the state of men and women who are not in right relationship with God. We turn to therapeutic counseling and prescriptions for help. Granted, our western culture has created overwhelming pressures and expectations for all of us, as well as a breakdown in the greatest "support group" ever created, the family. But can anyone justify how we Christians so often leave God and his Word out of the equation when we face all of the complexities that life brings our way? Is the slogan "God plus one equals a majority" *not* actually true? Is not God our greatest counselor, helper, and support in the midst of every imaginable struggle and trial?

2. Biblical Counseling–As alluded to above, I believe that the primary premise that should guide and motivate the disciple investor lies in the conviction that the Bible, the Word of God, is fully trustworthy and has the answers needed for both soul care and the ongoing sanctification process of believers. Therefore, the best solution for any personal, spiritual problem must be resourced from Scripture. The Bible is the most powerful prescription for answering the tough life–problems of the soul. Our problems usually arise from our sin, and our sin can only be solved by considering what God tells us. We must listen to him, look at his answers and respond accordingly. Life-transformation comes from interacting with the Scriptures and being led by the Holy Spirit.

3. Personal Application–Spiritual diagnosis inevitably reveals problems in people's lives. These problems arise from

their own sins and weaknesses and often derive from poor thinking. Hence, as disciple investors, we should function somewhat as counselors and strive to be "Bible teachers" as well. We want to address the real issues and provide biblical answers.

4. Dealing with Repentance: Transformational Living–Few doctrines receive less fanfare than the doctrine of repentance, i. e., the decision to turn from one's sin. Some Christian extremists relegate this doctrine to the Old Testament people of God, while others believe that the doctrine of repentance is contrary to faith and therefore ultimately a work that hinders salvation. Still others believe that it is a negative teaching that becomes too confused with penitence and self-reformation. Nevertheless, the doctrine is thoroughly biblical and needs to be "preached" to those who wish to follow Jesus. Jesus preached repentance (Luke 13:3, 5) and Paul submitted that the doctrine was a core feature of his gospel proclamation (Acts 20:21). Therefore, although not always easy, the faithful disciple investor needs to ask, "Is there anything in your life of which you need to repent?" "Are you willing to repent of your sin?"

## The Necessity of Follow-Up

Having provided prescription from God's Word, and sensing a hopeful application of the Scriptures to life, the disciple investor must recognize that some type of accountability ought to be involved in the process of Christian growth and sanctification. One of the great joys of the disciple investing process is the joy of follow-up. Meeting again with a new believer, possibly multiple times, is one of the great pleasures of life-investment. We have asserted that new believers need accountability, but in some ways they need the loving care of a regular, dependable relationship. In a relational context, spiritual growth can thrive.

New believers need to share their successes, failures, joys, and struggles in their new found Christian walk, and at the same time, these stories will bring blessings to the disciple investor. Follow-up reveals progress and struggle; it helps to continue the diagnostic ministry of the disciple investor. Blessing abounds when the disciple investor asks questions, listens to answers, hears testimonies, and shares wisdom. Investor and disciple grow together in the Lord and find mutually satisfying joy in their relationship!

## Love/Sexuality/Lust/Marriage

Here are four of the most powerful topics that need to be addressed in anyone and everyone's lives. Starting with the youngest child, these questions need to be addressed on some level. If love is the universal language (some think music is, but both certainly seem to go together), then understanding the nature of love (committed love) is essential for living in a godly and holy fashion. Here is an area that is most difficult to address, primarily due to the reality that love (however it might be defined) is both personal and powerful and has become a highly celebrated idol in western culture. We love our idols and we do not want another person to "mess" with them.

Idols, as you might know, can be shaped into whatever image an individual desires. That is what western culture has done with love: we have shaped love into an idol with little regard for God's perspective. In western culture, thinking God's thoughts (godliness) does not predominate in the areas of love, sex, lust, and sadly, marriage. Marriage, by biblical definition, is that committed relationship that occurs only between a consenting man and woman, making vows and promises before God and man (mankind) to remain faithful throughout life. Although this definition may not be the popular view in the United States, these issues and definitions regarding love and marriage must be discussed because pursuing the holy route in all matters of life is the goal of disciple investing. Love, as it is so powerful, must constantly be a topic of discussion in the life of the believer. The follower of Jesus always wants to discover how to please the Lord and glorify him, no matter what the cost.

Again, we are "messing" with a powerful idol, whether it is a man wishing to fulfill the desires of his extraordinary libido, or a woman whose passion is to cling to the man who makes her secure or happy (or vice-versa). To directly confront sin in this area always puts the disciple investing relationship at risk. Nevertheless, the disciple investor and disciple must explore, address, and deal with all sexual sin, heterosexual or homosexual; otherwise, holiness will not ensue. Of course, it begins with dealing with the area of lust, i.e., sinful passion for any sexual activity outside of the will of God. Lust starts in the mind and the heart. Its power, if unrepressed, has the ability to overtake the will, ending in sinful acts. One must repent of lust early and quickly. All sexual lust habits, whether viewing inappropriate media (enticing movies, television, internet sites, videos, etc.), reading provocative literature or engaging in pornographic activities that spawn negative practices, eventually reap devastating personal and relational consequences.

Abdicating to one's personal sins leads to sexual addictions or in more biblical terms, enslavement to sin and its unyielding grip. Addictions become idols and idols, without God's help, are impossible to release or destroy. Ultimately, in the area of sexuality and lust (subsets of love and marriage), we are dealing with realities of the heart. An empty, fallen, and broken heart leads to attempts to fulfill ungodly desires. The disciple investor will do well to focus on the heart of the disciple, move him to both rely upon the gospel, and deal honestly and openly with his sexual struggles. Christ-focused confession and repentance brings relief but confession will only arise as the issue of sexuality and its struggles are frankly and directly addressed. Thinking upon and discussing these powerful issues precedes confession and confession (with repentance) leads to freedom.

## Words and Language

Some of the best conversations I have had with new believers (or spiritually responsive unbelievers) are those in which the new believer uses language that is not always socially appropriate (what was once considered "crass" language is now much more completely acceptable culturally and socially). In some ways, nothing is more refreshing than hearing a person freely use, in your presence, what appear to be the most inappropriate words, whether those are curse words, profanity, or blasphemy of some sort. If someone feels free to use such words, you have probably built a bridge of transparency with them. Speaking from experience, there is probably nothing much more awkward or embarrassing than to have a person apologize profusely for foul language to the extent that it completely evades the heart issue. While trying to avoid a legalistic mentality that ranks all types of inappropriate language on a relative scale (I personally see no need for using any of them and try to let my "yes be yes" and my "no be no"), thus making some worse than others (and some are worse than others), I *do* think that the use (or misuse) of language is indicative of a person's state of heart. Jesus said so in Luke 6:45, "The good person out of the good treasure of his heart produces good, and the evil person out of his evil treasure produces evil, for out of the abundance of the heart his mouth speaks."

The reality is that profane speech tends to come from a profane heart. All that being said, I expect to hear this type of language (yes, sometimes I hear apologies along with it) when I engage in honest and open conversations with those who are in the beginning stages of their growth in Christ. My personal view is that I simply start where they are and don't even address the language problem. There is one exception: misuse of the name of God–if I have opportunity, I will tell the other person that they are defaming a holy name and breaking one of the Ten Commandments. Otherwise, I want to focus on the issues of the heart, recognizing that biblically speaking, by dealing with heart issues as a primary focus, the nature of what exits the mouth will be changed in time as well.

One hope of the disciple investing process is that the person being discipled will grow in sanctified conversation to the glory of God. Some might wish to build a case for the proper use of profane language or statements, but I see no use attempting to build that case, especially with new believers who usually wrestle more seriously with their own heart struggles and wish to depart or repent from their previous manner of living without Christ. My bottom line for this issue is to accept the person's language; however it is expressed (with the exception of misuse of God's name) as a natural reflection of the disciple's starting point in the sanctification process. Then I focus on heart change and watch the natural progress of Spirit-led change in language expression.

## Personal Stewardship: Financial Management and Time Management

The key to this important category lies in the word "personal." How are people doing in the daily stewardship of time and money? Like the area of sexuality, these areas of life are intensely personal. Rare is the individual who invites examination of personal practices in either of these areas of stewardship. Yet the question has to be addressed, at least to some extent. I do not think it is proper to pry into an individual's finances, but conceptually there are issues that need to be noted. Particularly, if the individual is married, the disciple investor ought to ask these questions. Money is the biggest stress in marriage and the biggest contributor to ongoing marital conflict. A husband and wife often see money in very different ways.

For high school students, it is appropriate to ask if they work or are making any money of their own. How do they purchase their necessities or pay for their hobbies and interests? Do they feel unduly dependent upon their parent or parents? For college students, one must ask whether or not they are going into debt for a college education. Do they have college loans and how much? Are they spending their money wisely? Are they working a job as they attend college or are they willing to slow down their degree track in order to govern their finances? How do they perceive that they might repay their loans? For adults or professionals, ask questions about indebtedness with credit cards particularly (auto loans add up as well). Address how to avoid those interest rates. Do they have a monthly budget based on income and specific expenses? Are they overpaying for an automobile (can they commit to a more affordable vehicle)? If married, have they worked out spending limits, balancing the checkbook and communicating about significant purchases? I might add that it never hurts to ask about giving or tithing and to discuss how that might look in any believer's or couple's life.

In some ways I think that accountability with money is much easier than accountability with time. Time use, however, does measure the priorities in our lives. We must ask the disciple, "When are you spending time with the Lord in some sort of prioritized devotional activity?" Similarly, if married we might ask "When are you spending time with your spouse in some sort of prioritized 'I am devoted to you' activity?" (Neither question should be interpreted as pushing a legalistic agenda.) "In what ways do you take time to minister to others, if any?" "How do you use your leisure time?" "Are you involved in any addictive activities that might waste your time or any activities that might cause you to use your time poorly?" "How might you use your time better?" "What are your top priorities and how could your time better reflect your priorities?"

## Decisions and Choices Made in Life

No matter what age, most people look back at their lives and without fail, due to their sins or simply some very bad decisions and choices, realize that they must face the present based on the past. A genuinely interested disciple investor should never hesitate to discover if the disciple has any regrets. The failures and poor decisions of the past cannot be changed but the disciple investor must encourage the follower of Christ to understand that God is sovereign and that he can redeem our bad past decisions, using them to work his good and perfect will in the lives of his people.

## The Importance of Words of Affirmation

Simply stated, any time you as a disciple investor meet with aspiring disciples, whether they respond positively or negatively to your time together, you need to express the desire that you want to meet again. No matter what deep sins they may have confessed, or negative reactions they may have expressed, you know that a long-term relationship, if the Lord allows it, will only benefit both parties. You are their servant to minister to them in any way possible; thus you know that retaining the relationship allows an ongoing context of ministry. Disciple investing means friendship and friendship thrives where proper and honest affirmation dwell. The healthy disciple investor makes it clear that she wants to continue the relationship with the disciple and that, no matter how difficult or uncomfortable the initial encounter may have been, she wishes to foster a continuing relationship, truly believing that indeed "God is at work!"

## SAMPLE DIAGNOSTIC-TYPE QUESTIONS

Asking diagnostic questions is an art. As mentioned previously, the questions themselves comprise the science. However, the art comes through use and practice. A disciple investor must develop good question asking skills; it must become a mentality of ministry. Listening is an art as well. The art of question asking also demands that the disciple investor demonstrates acceptable relational skills and abilities. The art may come more naturally to conversationalists but they can lose focus also. They can talk too much and become focused on their own thoughts and agenda. The science involves knowing the questions. The art revolves around developing the relationship, i.e., building bridges, asking questions, listening and being genuinely interested, and responsive. A sense of self-sacrifice and investing in others is another necessary premium. The art includes taking time to listen, knowing when to ask questions, and knowing what questions are appropriate given the setting and the context of the conversation.

For the purpose and benefit of the science of diagnosis (or asking questions), I have compiled this list of questions over the years to help others know where to begin in the ministry of "questioning." These three lists of questions should assist you in discovering how others think, feel, or behave, and include personal spiritual/soul diagnostics for basic marriage counseling questions.

## General Questions

1. Evangelism Explosion (EE) Questions (I believe that these questions are almost always poignant and relevant no matter what a person says they believe or don't believe about God or heaven):

    Question # 1: Have you come to the place in your spiritual life/ thinking that you know for certain that if you were to die tonight, you would go to heaven?

    Question # 2: If you were to die tonight and God were to say to you, "Why should I let you into my heaven?" what would you say?

2. What type of church/spiritual background do you have?

3. What do you think God is like?

4. What does (or what do you think) the Bible say(s) about God?

5. Did your church (growing up) teach from the Bible? What was your church/pastor's view of the Bible?

6. Did you ever have a time in your life (growing up) in which you made a commitment to Christ or the church? Tell me about it. . . .

7. What is your most significant religious/spiritual experience?

8. Who is Jesus to you?

9. What was your family life/relation to parents (mom/dad) like?

10. What problems do your friends experience?

11. How do you get over problems/failures/struggles in your life?

12. What really makes you mad?

13. I really have a problem with _____. (This statement opens the door through identification with another person's possible problem– lust, anger, bitterness, loneliness, rejection, materialism, etc.)

14. Who are your friends? What are they like?

15. Have you seen any good movies/read any good books lately?

16. What hurts you most? What causes you pain?

17. What motivates you (or de-motivates you)?

18. How does your thought life bother you? (Crazy or bizarre thoughts?)

19. What kinds of sin enter your thought life?

## Soul/Heart Searching Questions

1. How is/are your family (parents/siblings) doing?

2. How are all of your relationships (girlfriend/boyfriend/marriage) going?

3. How is life at school or work?

4. How is your (and family members') health?

5. Do you feel like things are going well for you? (or) Do you have any struggles in your life? With what do you struggle?

6. What are the challenges you are experiencing in life these days?

7. In what ways are you learning to trust the Lord?

8. Are you learning anything new about God, or your relationship with God?

9. Is there any way in which you sense you are growing spiritually?

10. Do you enjoy serving in your/any ministry capacity? What causes that enjoyment?

11. Are there any new ministries in which you would like to be involved?

12. How is your devotional life?

13. Do you try to have spiritual discussions with your roommate or friends?

14. Has the Lord taught you anything new about yourself recently?

15. How do the Scriptures or the gospel apply to your situation?

## Counseling

"Counseling is simply teaching the Scriptures on a one-to-one basis."–The late Buck Hatch, Professor at Columbia International University, Columbia, South Carolina.

Questions/Issues for Marriage and Relational Counseling: *Note:* these are the areas that I explore particularly when engaging with couples seriously thinking about or planning to be married.

1.  Define love (1Corinthians 13, Ephesians 4:32, John 15:9-17).

2.  Tell me about your respective families, your background, and your upbringing.

3.  What are your respective temperaments and differences? Use the following personality profiles and discuss them as able:

    A.  The DISC (couples must pay for this profile)

    B.  Myers-Briggs (available on the internet in multiple locations)

4.  How do you handle your anger? (Issues: Anger expression, management and control, and resolution)

5.  What do you see as the fundamental differences between men and women? (Discuss Dr. Larry Crabb's views: Women want security and men want significance–do you agree or disagree and why?)

6.  Roles, Responsibilities, and Tasks–Work and Home: What are your views of women and men, and the role of work in the home and outside the home for both husband and wife?

7.  Biblical Mandates for Marriage and Their Application: Ephesians 5

    A.  Husband: Love his wife as Christ loved the church and gave himself for her

    B.  Wife: Submission in the Lord

8.  Conflict and Conflict Resolution

9.  Money Management

    A.  Spending and saving differences in personality; control and spending

    B.  Budget creation and management (balancing)

    C.  Debt

    D. Retirement, investments, and annuities

    E. Health, death, and disability insurance

    F. Materialism and living simply

10. Sexual Expectations

    A. Past Experiences

    B. Present Physical Relationship

    C. Initiation and communication

    D. Sexual pleasure

    E. Birth Control

    F. The Problem of Pornography

11. Children

    A. Planning

    B. Number

    C. Child raising styles and method

    D. Issues of child discipline

12. Communication–Listening and Responding

13. Time Management

    A. Mornings and evenings

    B. Scheduling meals, time together, family and personal devotions

    C. Social life and friends

    D. Personal space and private time

## Questions for Reflection

1. What was the most helpful section of this chapter?

2. What do you think about using questions in order to discover (or diagnose) another person's understanding of scriptural teachings? What are this methodology's strengths and weaknesses?

3. What is the difference between the *science* of asking "soul searching" questions and the *art* of asking "soul searching" questions? How does a disciple investor move from the science to the art?

4. Which of the five "Purposes of Spiritual Diagnosis" resonates the most with you?

## Action Points

1. Read through the list of "Sample-Type Diagnostic Questions" one more time. Choose three that you think would be useful in your ministry of disciple investing.

2. Ask a couple of friends if you can "experiment" with them by practicing some of the diagnostic questions on them.

# 8

# Areas of Disciple Investing

IF YOU ARE LOOKING for Scripture passages that you could use in a disciple investing relationship, I have provided a number of helpful topics and areas of concern, along with appropriate Bible texts, below. Each of these topics is relevant to the Christian life and should be addressed from a biblical perspective (as much as is possible) with appropriate application to the individual believer's life. Remember that you, as the disciple investor, should use the skill of diagnosis to discover needs of the disciple, both in heart and understanding. The most effective method of addressing a specific topic would be to find a Bible passage (just one, if possible) that addresses the topic and to walk through the passage with the other person. I would suggest that you, as disciple investor, should use a method that is known as the modified inductive Bible study. All that means is that together you ask questions of the text and try to interpret it as best as you are able (this is when it is necessary for you do a little reading or study to help with understanding; then you follow up with the easiest and most fun part, i.e., applying the text to yourself, the disciple, and the contemporary world–life issues we are facing today). At times, of course, multiple passages and cross references are helpful or needed in order to adequately explore and understand the respective topics.

Below is a list of topics and Scripture passages that would address each topic and assist in its study.

## Living the Christian Life

- *Assurance (of Salvation)*–John 1:9–13; Romans 8:14–17; 1 John 5:11–13

- *Authority (Dealing with) and Submission*–Luke 1:26–38; Romans 13:1–7

- *Christian Liberty*–Romans 14:1–12; 14:13–23; 1 Corinthians 6:12–20; 8 (whole chapter); 10:23–33; Galatians 5:1–15

- *Compassion*–Matthew 9:35–10:8 (9:36); 15:29–32

- *Commitment (A committed life)*–Luke 9:57–62; 14:25–35

- *Contentment*–Exodus 20:17; (Romans 7:7–12); Philippians 4:10–20

- *Faith/Trust*–Hebrews 11; 1 John 5:1–5

- *Faithfulness*–Joshua 24:14–28; Psalm 51:1–6; 3 John 1:1–8

- *Fear of the Lord*–Exodus 19:1–25; 20:18–21; Hebrews 12:18–29

- *Fellowship*–Hebrews 10:24–25

- *Fighting Sin*–Colossians 3:1–14

- *Filling of the Holy Spirit*–Galatians 5:13–26; Ephesians 5:15–21 (18)

- *Forgiveness*–Psalm 51; 130:3–4; Isaiah 1:1–20 (18); Micah 7:18–19; Matthew 18:21–35; Ephesians 4:31–32; 1 John 1:6–2:2

- *Fruit of the Spirit*–Galatians 5:13–26

- *Giving (Tithing)*–Malachi 3:1–10; 2 Corinthians 8:1–15; 9:6–15

- *Grace*–1 Corinthians 15:1–10; Ephesians 2:1–10

- *Gratitude (Thankfulness)*–Psalm 100; 1 Thessalonians 5:16–18; 1 Timothy 4:1–4

- *Growth (of the Believer)*–Ephesians 4:11–16; Colossians 1:9–14; 1:28–2:8

- *The Heart and Heart Attitudes*–1 Samuel 16:1–13; Matthew 15:1–20

- *Holiness/Purity*–1 John 3:1–10; 1 Peter 1:13–21

- *Identity "in Christ"*–Romans 6:1–23; Ephesians 1:3–14

- *Idols and Idolatry*–Exodus 20:1–6; Ezekiel 14:1–11; 1 John 5:20–21

- *Integrity*–Psalm 26:1–3, 10–12; 101:1–3; Proverbs 10:8–10

- *Joy*–Philippians 4:4–19; Psalm 100
- *Justification (and the Believer)*–Romans 5:1–21; Galatians 2:15–21
- *Leisure*–Proverbs 6:6–11, 26:13–16; Colossians 3:1–4, 17; Ephesians 5:8–20
- *Lies (The World's Deceit)*–1 John 2:18–27
- *Lordship of Christ*–Romans 9:10–13; Colossians 1:9–20
- *Love*–John 13:31–35; 1 John 4:7–21
- *Loving God*–Deuteronomy 6:1–6; 11:1–25; Matthew 22:34–39; 1 John 4:7–21
- *Loving People*–Leviticus 19:1–18; Matthew 22:34–39; 1 John 4:7–21
- *Maturity/Christ-likeness*–Ephesians 4:11–16; Colossians 1:24–29; James 1:1–7
- *Meditation, Christian*–Joshua 1:1–9; Psalm 1; 19; 119:14–16
- *Money and Possessions (Materialism)*–1 Timothy 6:3–19; Luke 16:12–15
- *Obedience*–1 Samuel 15:1–31; Isaiah 1:10–20; John 14:15–24
- *Peace of God*–Isaiah 26:1–4; Philippians 4:1–9 (6–7); Colossians 3:15
- *Perseverance*–Hebrews 10:32–39; 12:1–3; James 1:1–5
- *Personal Rights*–1 Corinthians 9:1–23
- *Personal Discipline*–1 Corinthians 9:24–27; 2 Timothy 2:1–6; Titus 2:11–15
- *Personal Devotions (Quiet Time)*–Psalm 5:1–8; 42; Matthew 6:5–8; Mark 1:29–39
- *Prayer*–Ezra 9; Nehemiah 9; Matthew 6:1–13
- *Pride*–Ezekiel 28:11–19; Obadiah 1:1–9; 1 Peter 5:5–11
- *Purpose and Meaning*–Deuteronomy 10:12–22; Ecclesiastes 2:1–26; John 10:1–10
- *Purpose of the Christian Life*–Romans 8:26–30; 1 Corinthians 10:31; Ephesians 1:11–14; 4:17–24; 1 Peter 2:9–12
- *Rat Race, The*–1 Kings 11:1–13; Ecclesiastes 2:17–26; Luke 12:13–21

- *Reconciliation*–Romans 5:1–11; 2 Corinthians 5:16–6:2; Matthew 5:21–26

- *Repentance*–Isaiah 55:1–7; Luke 13:1–5; 2 Corinthians 7:8–12

- *Responsibility*–1 Samuel 17:17–37; 2 Timothy 2:19–30

- *Rest*–Mark 6:30–36

- *Sabbath (Understanding)*–Exodus 20:8; Nehemiah 13:1–22; Isaiah 58:12–14; Hebrews 4:1–11

- *Sanctification*–Romans 7:14–25; 8:1–17

- *Sacrifice*–Romans 12:1–2; 2 Corinthians 4:7–18; Ephesians 5:1–2; Philippians 2:19–30

- *Satan (Dealing With)*–Genesis 3:1–15; Zechariah 3:1–2; Matthew 4:1–11; 2 Corinthians 2:12–15; Ephesians 6:10–12; James 4:6–8; 1 Peter 5 (especially verses 7–9)

- *Service (Servanthood)*–Mark 10:44–45; John 13:1–20; Galatians 5:13–18

- *Sex and Sexual Morality*–Matthew 5:27–30; 1 Corinthians 6:9–20; Ephesians 5:3–13; Colossians 3:1–11; 1 Thessalonians 4:1–8

- *Scriptures, The (Bible)*–Psalm 19; 119; Luke 24:13–35; 2 Timothy 3; 2 Peter 1:12–21

- *Self-denial*–Luke 9:21–26; 1 Corinthians 9:19–23

- *Sin*–Jeremiah 17:5–10; Romans 3:9–20; Ephesians 2:1–5

- *Spiritual Disciplines*–See Scriptures, Reading and Study, Prayer, Personal Devotions, Giving, Fasting, Service

- *Spiritual Gifts*–Romans 12:3–8; I Corinthians 12:1–31; Ephesians 4:7–16; I Peter 4:7–11

- *Spiritual Warfare*–Ephesians 6:10–20

- *Stewardship*–Luke 19:11–26

- *Submission*–Proverbs 3:1–6; Romans 13:1–7; Ephesians 5:21–33; Hebrews 13:15–17

- *Success (Handling)*—Deuteronomy 8; 1 Kings 10:1–9; 11:1–14; Matthew 16:26

- *Suffering*–Job 19:21–27; Isaiah 53; Romans 5:1–11; 8:18–30; 2 Corinthians 12:1–10; 1 Peter 4:12–19

- *Temptation*–Matthew 4:1–11; 1 Corinthians 10:1–13; Hebrews 2:14–18; James 1:12–18

- *Time Management*–Psalm 39:4–6; 90:1–17; Ecclesiastes 3:1–11; Romans 13:11–14; Galatians 6:9–10; Ephesians 5:8–20 (16)

- *Tongue, The*–Ephesians 4:20–32; 5:1–7; James 3:1–12; 4:11–12

- *Trials*–Job 19:21–27; Jeremiah 15:15–21; 1 Thessalonians 3:1–4; James 1:1–18; 1 Peter 1:1–9

- *Will of God, The*–Psalm 37:1–6; Romans 12:1–2; 1 Corinthians 2:12–13; Ephesians 5:8–21 (17)

- *Work*–Genesis 2:4–17; Nehemiah 4; Ephesians 4:28; Colossians 3:22–24; 1 Thessalonians 2:8–10; 4:10–12; 2 Thessalonians 3:7–11

- *Worship*–Psalm 95; John 4:19–26; Revelation 4:1–11; 15:1–4

- *World, The (Relating to)*–John 16:1–11; 17:6–19; 1 John 2:15–17

- *World and Life View*–Romans 12:2; 1 Corinthians 2:4–10; 2 Corinthians 10:4–6; Colossians 1:18

## Personal Concerns

- *Aging*–Deuteronomy 4:21–40 (Moses' reminiscing); Ecclesiastes 12:1–8; Isaiah 3:1–5

- *Alcohol (Addiction and Drunkenness)*–Proverbs 23:29–35; Ephesians 5:15–20

- *Ambition*–Romans 15:19–21; Philippians 2:3–11,19–30; James 3:13–15

- *Anger*–Exodus 2:11–15; 32:1–35; Numbers 20:1–13; Proverbs 15:1; 29:8; Matthew 21:12–17; Mark 3:1–6; Ephesians 4:25–31; Colossians 3:7–9; James 1:19–20

- *Anxiety/Worry*–Proverbs 3:5–6; Matthew 6:25–34; Luke 10:38–42; 12:22–34; Philippians 4:6–7; 1 Peter 5:6–7

- *Change (Hope For)*–Luke 5:1–11; 8:1–15,26–39; 2 Corinthians 5:16–21

- *Conflict*–Proverbs 6:12–14,19; 10:12; 15:18; 16:28; 28:25; 29:22; Luke 6:1–11; Acts 15:36–41

- *Death*–Psalm 49; 90; John 5:19–30; Philippians 1:19–26 (21); 2 Timothy 4:1–8

- *Depression*–1 Kings 19:1–18; Psalm 32; 143; Philippians 4:10–20 (Paul in prison)

- *Disappointment*–Habakkuk 1–3

- *Discouragement*–Psalm 42; 43; 2 Corinthians 4:7–18

- *Doubt*–Psalm 13; 73; Mark 9:14–29; Luke 24:36–43; John 20:19–31; Romans 4:18–22; Hebrews 11:8–12

- *Failure (and Restoration)*–Psalm 51; Luke 9:25; 22:1–34 (32), 39–62; John 21:15–23; (Acts 2:14,36; 1 Peter 5:1–4)

- *Favoritism*–James 2:1–13

- *Fear*–Isaiah 41:1–14; Matthew 8:23–27; 2 Timothy 1:3–14; 1 John 4:18–19

- *Grief*–Psalm 6; 56:8; Isaiah 53; John 11:17–37

- *Guilt*–Psalm 32; 38; 51 (based on 2 Samuel 11 and 12:1–15)

- *Loneliness*–Genesis 2:19–25; 2 Timothy 4:9–18; Colossians 3:1–4

- *Lust*–Numbers 15:38–40; 2 Samuel 11:1–27; Proverbs 6:20–35; Matthew 5:27–30; Romans 1:21–31; Colossians 3:4–6; James 1:12–18; 1 John 2:15–17

- *Lying and Denial*–Exodus 20:16; Psalm 5; Zephaniah 3:9–13

- *Personal Goals, Dreams, Hopes for Life*–Genesis 15:1–21; Psalm 1; Matthew 6:19–34 (33); Ephesians 3:14–21; Philippians 3:12–21

- *Performance (and Expectations)*–Nehemiah 6:1–16; Philippians 3:1–14

- *Priorities*–Ecclesiastes 12; Matthew 6:25–34; Philippians 3:12–21; Colossians 3:1–4

- *Self-concept/esteem and Insecurity*–Genesis 1:26–27; Exodus 3; Psalm 8:1–8 (3–8); Jeremiah 1:4–10, 17–19; Romans 8:14ff; 2 Timothy 1:3–10; 1 Peter 1:18–19

- *Self-infliction*–Matthew 22:37–40; 1 Corinthians 6:12–20

- *Singleness*–1 Corinthians 7
- *Stress*–Joshua 1:1–11

## Evangelism and Discipleship

- *Defining the Gospel*–Luke 23:38–43; Acts 2:22–41; 7:1–52; 10:34–43; 13:16–52; 17:22–34; 20:21; 1 Corinthians 15:1–11; 2 Corinthians 5:17–21; Colossians 1:15–23; Philippians 2:5–11
- *Disciple Investing*–Matthew 4:18–22; 2 Timothy 2:1–4; Acts 9:23–30; 16:1–5; 17:1–4; Acts 17:10–15; 18:24–28; 19:1–10; 20:1–6,13–37; Galatians 2:1; 4:8–19; Ephesians 1:15–23; 3:14–21
- *Evangelism*–Isaiah 6:1–13; Matthew 9:35–38; John 10:14–18; Romans 10:1–21; 2 Corinthians 2:12–17; Colossians 4:2–6; 1 Peter 3:13–16
- *Great Commission*–Genesis 12:1–3 (3); Psalm 67; 96; Isaiah 42:1–7; Matthew 28:18–20; Acts 1:1–11 (8)
- *Personal Testimony*–John 4:39–42; 9:13–29; Acts 26:1–23
- *Scripture Memorization*–Deuteronomy 18:16–20 (18); Psalm 40:6–8; 119:9–11; Matthew 4:1–11; Colossians 3:15–17
- *Ten Commandments, The (Guide for Living)*–Exodus 20

## Doctrine and Theology

- *Baptism*–Matthew 28:18–20; Acts 2:29–41 (38, 41); Colossians 2:11–13
- *Church, The*–Acts 2:41–47; 1 Corinthians 12:12–31; Ephesians 2:11–22; Colossians 1:18
- *Sacraments*–See Baptism, Communion (Lord's Supper)
- *CHRIST*
- *Person*–John 1:1–18; 14:6–14; Colossians 1:15–23; 2:9–15; Hebrews 1:1–9
- *Work*–2 Corinthians 5:16–21; Colossians 1:15–23; 2:9–15; 1 John 2:1–2
- *Resurrection*–Matthew 28; 1 Corinthians 6:12–17; 15:1–58

- *Return*–John 14:1–6; Acts 1:1–11; 1 Thessalonians 4:14–18; 2 Thessalonians 1:5–10

- *Judge*–John 5:16–30; Revelation 20:11–15

- *In the Old Testament*–Genesis 3:13–15; Isaiah 53:1–54:1; Psalm 2; Psalm 22

- *Ethics (Ten Commandments, The: Guide for Living)*–Exodus 20; Deuteronomy 5

- *GOD'S CHARACTER*

- *Creator*–Genesis 1:1ff; Romans 1:18–23

- *Eternal*–Exodus 3:1–14; Psalm 90:1–12

- *Faithfulness (Truth)*–Numbers 23:13–20; Lamentations 3:19–24

- *Glory*–Exodus 16:7–10; 24:12–18; 33:17–23; 34:4–8; John 1:14, 18

- *Goodness*–Exodus 34:5–7; Nehemiah 9:5–38; Psalm 119:65–72; Romans 2:4–5

- *Grace*–1 Corinthians 15:3–10; Ephesians 2:1–10

- *Holy*–Psalm 99:1–11; Isaiah 6:1–10

- *Infinite/Omnipresent*–Psalm 139:7–12; Jeremiah 23:23–24; Acts 17:24–28

- *Jealousy*–Exodus 20:1–5; 34:10–14

- *Just*–Matthew 25:31–46; 2 Corinthians 5:6–10; Revelation 20:11–15

- *Love*–Jeremiah 30:1–31:4; Romans 8:35–39; Hebrews 12:5–12; 1 John 4:7–21

- *Mercy*–Psalm 103:8–14; 1 Timothy 1:12–17

- *Omniscient (All-knowing)*–Psalm 139:1–6, 13–16

- *Omnipotent (Power)*–Jeremiah 32:16–29; Daniel 4:24–35; Hebrews 1:3

- *Patience*–Exodus 34:5–8; 1 Timothy 1:12–17; 1 Peter 3:18–20; 2 Peter 3:8–15

- *Personal (Spirit)*–Psalm 94:5–11; John 4:21–26

- *Sovereign*–Genesis 20:15–21; Isaiah 44:24–28; Ephesians 1:5–12

- *Triune (Trinity)*–Matthew 3:13–16; 28:18–20; John 8:48–58; 2 Corinthians 13:14; Ephesians 4:4–7; 1 Peter 1:2; Jude 20–21

- *Unchangeable (Immutable)*–1 Timothy 6:11–16; James 1:16–18

- *Wise*–1 Corinthians 1:18–30

- *Wrath/Anger*–Isaiah 64:1–11; Hebrews 10:26–39

- *Holy Spirit (Person and Work)*–John 14:15–27; 15:26–27; 16:12–15; Romans 8:1–17, 22–26; 1 Corinthians 3:16–17; Ephesians 1:11–14; 1 Thessalonians 1:4–10

- *Kingdom of God/Heaven*–Matthew 5:1–12; 13:24–35, 47–52

- *MAN*

- *Fall of Man*–Genesis 3:1–24; Romans 5:12–21; 2 Corinthians 11:1–4 (3)

- *Image of God*–Genesis 1:26–31; Genesis 9:1–7; Colossians 3:5–11 (10); James 3:1–12 (9)

- *Nature of Sin*–Jeremiah 17:5–10 (9); Romans 3:9–20; Ephesians 2:1–5; 2 Timothy 3:1–9

- *SALVATION*

- *Conversion*–John 3:1–15; Acts 9:1–20

- *Justification*–Romans 4; 5:1–11 (12–21); 7:14–8:4; 8:28–30; 1 Corinthians 6:9–11; Galatians 2:15–20; 3:1–14; Philippians 3:7–9; Titus 3:3–8 (6)

- *Adoption*–John 1:12–13; Romans 8:14–17; 9:6–9; Galatians 4:1–7; Ephesians 1:3–7; 1 John 3:1–3

- *Redemption*–1 Peter 1:13–21; 2:21–25; Romans 3:21–26

- *Sanctification*–John 17:13–18; Romans 8; Colossians 3:1–17; 1 Thessalonians 4:1–8; 5:16–24 (23); 1 John 3:1–10

- *Glorification*–Romans 8:28–30; 1 Corinthians 15:51–58; Philippians 3:7–14; 1 John 3:1–3; Revelation 21; 22

- *Satan (Who is He?)*–Job 1:1–12; Matthew 13:38–40; John 8:42–47; 2 Corinthians 2:5–11; 1 Peter 5:7–9; 1 John 3:7–10

- *Second Coming of Christ*–Matthew 24; 1 Thessalonians 4:13–18; 2 Thessalonians 1:5–12; 2:1–12

- *Sin*–Romans 3:9–20; Ephesians 2:1–5

## Relationships

- *Dating (and Love)*–Proverbs 7; 1 Corinthians 10:23–33; 13; 2 Corinthians 6:14–18; 1 Thessalonians 4:3–5; 2 Timothy 2:20–22; 1 Peter 2:9–12
- *Friendship*–1 Samuel 18:1–4; Proverbs 17:17; 18:24; 27:6, 17; Ecclesiastes 4:9–12; John 15:9–17
- *Marriage*–Genesis 2:18–25; Proverbs 5:1–23; 6:20–35; 18:22; Malachi 2:10–16; Matthew 19:2–9; 1 Corinthians 7:1–25; 1 Corinthians 13; Ephesians 5:22–33; Colossians 3:18–19; Hebrews 13:4
- *Men and Women/Roles*–Genesis 1:26–31; 3:1–24; Proverbs 31; 1 Corinthians 11:1–3; Galatians 3:26–29; Ephesians 5:21–33; 1 Timothy 2:11–15; 1 Peter 3:1–7
- *Parenting (How To)*–Deuteronomy 6:1–25; Proverbs 1:8–19; 13:24; 19:18–19; 22:6; 23:13; 29:15, 17; Ephesians 6:1–4; Colossians 3:20–21
- *"One Another" Passages*–John 13:14, 34; Romans 12:10; 12:16; 14:13; 15:5, 7, 14; 16:6; Galatians 5:13, 26; 6:2; Ephesians 4:2, 32; 5:19; Colossians 3:13, 16; 1 Thessalonians 5:11; Hebrews 3:13; 10:24–25; James 4:11; 5:16; 1 Peter 4:9; 5:5; 1 John 1:7
- *Relationships (General)*–Matthew 18:21–35; 22:34–40; Romans 1:26–27; 1 Corinthians 13; 2 Corinthians 6:3–13; Titus 2:1–15; 1 John 2:3–11
- *Relating to Parents*–Exodus 20:12; Ephesians 6:1–4; Colossians 3:20

## Questions for Reflection

1. What are the topics, in the various lists above, that interest (or jump out at) you the most?

2. Looking over the list, take a little time and choose what you think would be the "Top Ten" most important topics for a *new* believer in Christ to understand.

3. Looking over the list, take a little time and choose what you think would be the "Top Ten" most important topics for a teenage Christian to understand.

4. Looking over the list, take a little time and choose what you think would be the "Top Ten" most important topics for an adult male (or a female) believer in Christ to understand.

## Action Points

1. Choose 3–5 of the areas in the list above and read the passages that help the disciple investor address the area of need.

2. After you read those passages, write down a few questions that you think would help you and another person explore the specific passage and learn God's will from it.

# 9

## Case Studies

THIS CHAPTER CONTAINS SOME short descriptions of possible scenarios that could (or did) occur to my knowledge, or in my experiences of disciple investing over the years. Some of the stories are mine, while others are stories I have seen or heard and know about. And there are also some stories in which either creative license or fictitious names have been used in order to maintain anonymity of the individuals and events described.

### Kim

Kim became a Christian through the ministry of Coral Ridge Presbyterian Church in the late 1970s. She was in her early twenties and single, and visited the church out of curiosity since its large building and high, upward spire made the facility stand out while driving by it on the North Federal Highway (US 1). After her visit, she received an in-home (or "in-apartment" in her case) non-appointment visit from three members of the church. They were part of a group of Coral Ridge members who had joined the Tuesday evening *Evangelism Explosion* team, a method of church visitor follow up that shares the gospel intentionally on the first home visit. Upon hearing the gospel explained that night, Kim asked Jesus Christ to be her Lord and Savior, and eventually joined Coral Ridge. However, right after she became a Christian, she was initially discipled in the most unusual circumstances. An older man in the church heard about her profession of faith and in some ways, not knowing better, he said to Kim, "Here, I have a great book for you to read. It will be very helpful." The book was entitled, *Evangelism and the Sovereignty of God* by Dr. J.I. Packer. Kim later said to me, "That really isn't the place to start as a new Christian, but I read the book and it made me see how great a God we have. That motivated me to get going in the Christian life and impacted me greatly." I might add that, to my knowledge, that man didn't disciple Kim any further. He just gave her a gift–a book that should have been "over her head" on a topic that some people don't even want to read about. That's all he did and God used it greatly in her life. Disciple investing sometimes doesn't take much–just a little interest, initiative, and implementation (giving away a book). He didn't even get involved. God took over from there and Kim grew spiritually from that point because Jesus was discipling her in his own way. He can use our worse or most unwise efforts for his own glory.

# Jared

Jared became a Christian a few years out of college through some friends he had met at work. Jared was excited about his Christian faith and his wife, who had been a somewhat casual church goer, got motivated to seek the Lord as well. Jared heard about a small Bible believing Presbyterian church near his residence and he and his wife began to attend. The church was so new that it didn't yet have a building. But because the Bible was being preached there, they stayed and joined. One day the pastor invited Jared out to breakfast before work on a weekday. The pastor did this a few times. They just talked, enjoyed each other, and began to spend some time together in other venues. Jared was wide open to being taught and wanted to learn everything about Christ and the Christian life. In a few years, Jared became an elder in the church. However, shortly afterward, the pastor was called to another church and left. Jared was sad because the pastor had helped him so much. Jared once told me, "When I was a new Christian, I started meeting with the pastor. We talked about everything. I was new and young. I didn't realize it at the time but the pastor was discipling me all the way through our time together!" He shook his head with wonder. Being discipled without even knowing it–*that* is disciple investing at its best!

## Taylor

Taylor attended a large state university and, like many freshmen, immediately struggled with all of the adjustments required to succeed. He was certain that he would fail out of college. He had a rough first semester but survived. In the spring semester of that freshman year, he found a group of Christian students known as Campus Crusade for Christ (now "Cru"). He had met some of the students at church. He was still struggling in his personal life and occasionally thought about giving up, or even about committing suicide at times. But one of the Cru students asked him to join his small group Bible study. Taylor really liked the other student and could tell that he was on fire for the Lord, so he joined. The group was only four or five guys, and together they would study the Bible. However, all of the students were very open about their struggles, something Taylor didn't expect. It was so refreshing for Taylor to see that he wasn't alone in his own personal struggles, that one night he opened up to the other guys about his sense of failure and the pressures he was facing. He wept intensely and although embarrassed at doing so, all of the other guys took it in stride and simply prayed for him. If you were to ask Taylor today what the Bible study was about that semester, he probably doesn't remember. But he probably can tell you the names of the guys who attended the study and how they helped support him in some of his lowest moments. Disciple investing includes content, doctrine, and study. But it also meets emotional needs and supports the other person in his trials and struggles.

## Frank

Frank was a very successful businessman and a leader in the church. As a church elder he was respected in the community, the church, and the business world. He and his wife opened their home for all of the youth groups to meet–middle schoolers, high schoolers, college and career–making it available, if they wanted to have a church event. His home was large but modest and since it had a swimming pool, lots of social gatherings were held there. Although a busy man, as one can imagine, Frank was known for singling out various individuals to see how they were doing in their life, business, or marriage. As an elder, he believed that he should show personal interest to the people under his care. The church pastor also was very pastoral and shepherded his people well. Nevertheless, Frank served in a complementary role to the pastor and he specialized in looking out for the disenfranchised, i.e., the elderly, the lonely, and those struggling financially. He loved the broken and would take care of them. His ministry wasn't one of spending a lot of one-to-one time with others, but it was one of looking out for the overlooked in both the church and the community. There is no telling how many lives he influenced and how many hurting people he encouraged. Although a very busy man, he found time to make others his business. Disciple investing means reaching out to others in need and speaking a timely word into their lives. It means making yourself available even when it appears that you should be unavailable.

## Hudson

As a teenager, Hudson took a summer job working for his father as a full-time day laborer in his father's large sheet metal factory. His father was president and partial owner of the company and a strong, committed Christian. Hudson was a believer in Christ, having grown up in such a solid Christian family. He was also overqualified for the job intellectually but he wanted to earn some of his own spending money, and working there was an improvement over sitting at home playing computer games. What he didn't realize was going to happen was that he would be assisting one of the other employees, Garrett, who was also there for a summer job. Garrett had already gone to and graduated from college and was working the summer job in the sheet metal factory in order to help him pay for graduate school. In some ways, Hudson shadowed Garrett in learning some basic skills but they also did a number of chores and tasks together, menial tasks that took very little strategic thinking. Lots of conversation, strung along with some good humor, would occur during these times. Garrett was very grateful for the job, as well as the income it generated. And as a committed Christian, knowing that a number of the other factory workers would be watching, he attempted to approach this "lowly" work with joy, enthusiasm, and vigor. As Hudson and Garrett walked around the grounds of the factory or travelled together for the delivery of materials to various homes and businesses, they would talk. Garrett never held a Bible study with Hudson, and they never actually prayed together, but their conversations would often turn to topics about the Christian life–particularly, how to be a committed Christian in the work place where not everyone believed or respected the Christian faith. Work ethic was an important emphasis in their discussions, as was the subject of a Christian's proper relationship with the opposite sex. Garrett discussed what being a Christian in college meant to him as well.

The summer went by quickly–the job lasted ten weeks or so–and Garrett moved on with his life. Every once in a while, though not often, he would run into Hudson, but time passed. About ten years later, however, Garrett ran into Hudson and his wife of a few years, along with some other friends, at a large convention sponsored by their denomination. They were very surprised, yet pleased to see each other, but the biggest surprise was Garrett's. After a warm, mutual greeting between the two men, Hudson turned to his friends and said, "Hey guys, I want you to meet my friend Garrett. Besides the influence of my father growing up, this man has impacted me today more than any other person." Garrett was amazed to hear these words and was certain that they were overstated. Nevertheless, that short summer of life was apparently quite the summer of disciple investing, although the time together was never strategic, purposeful, nor structured. Disciple investing is sometimes simply life-on-life with another person, pointing them to Christ, and showing them by example how a Christian lives.

## Joanna

Joanna was attending the local Christian college when she met Carly through the church that she attended. Carly was a teenager who had come to know the Lord a few years earlier at a Franklin Graham Festival. Carly had joined the church, although it was not her family's church. A few of her middle school friends attended and her parents didn't seem to mind if she switched churches even though she was still a young teenager, obviously living at home. Joanna was very busy with school-related activities and in a serious relationship with a young man, to whom she was engaged, and who also attended the same Christian college. But she truly wanted to do some type of ministry while in the college. Although she considered volunteering with Young Life, she decided to focus on her local church. She soon began attending the youth meetings, with the approval of the youth director, who was an older, seasoned woman, as well as being a very dynamic woman whom all of the youth loved and respected. Joanna was able to get to know some of the teenage girls and eventually the youth director encouraged her to initiate a relationship with any of them that she wished. Her time was limited, but she really hit it off with Carly.

Carly had received very little serious Christian training at her previous church, so she was "all ears" when it came to understanding the Bible, learning Christian doctrine, and discovering the answers to so many life questions (especially those related to boys!) Joanna would meet with Carly on an almost weekly basis, sharing things that she was learning at college and just talking and listening, as Carly expressed her desires, hopes, and dreams. Sometimes a few other girls would join them and they even had an occasional sleepover just for fun. Joanna and Carly became very close over the last two years of Joanna's schooling and once Joanna and her fiancé got married, Carly considered them her "spiritual parents." Carly's life was deeply impacted and spiritually shaped by this fun relationship with a college student. Her youth director was extremely formative but without Joanna in her life, Carly wondered if she would have grown so much. Disciple investing takes time and focus, and can include fun and friendship. Investing can occur just by being available, looking for someone who wants help, and spending time talking about life from the standpoint of a Christian worldview. Investing could mean that you will eventually be considered a "spiritual parent," and nothing much more complimentary than that can be said about anyone.

## Keith

Keith was a struggling teenager who had some deep relational problems with his dad. His father had some drug dependency issues and because of his inconsistent behavior, the family's life was quite unstable. In order to survive, Keith became withdrawn, cherished being a loner, and obviously had very few friends at school or in his church. He threw himself into his favorite hobby, art and was captivated by painting, pencil drawings, and amateur photography. Art allowed him to stay at home, appear productive (which he was), and remain aloof from the crowd. He didn't mind since he would never be part of the cool, popular kids at school anyhow. Ricky, a member of Keith's church, had noticed that Keith seemed to be disappearing and withdrawing from everyone. He figured Keith was just a normal teenager, dropping out of church because it was irrelevant to him. Ricky wondered if there were anything he could do. However, even though he was a few years older than Keith and didn't know him very well, as a single male in his early twenties, he thought possibly he could make a difference in Keith's life. Ricky was quite nervous about contacting Keith, since they were a few years apart and had never really spoken. However, he summoned up the nerve and called him on the phone. Surprisingly Keith was willing to meet and they set up a time to get together on a late afternoon. Ricky spent the first visit simply getting to know Keith and asking questions about his life, school, church, and especially about his hobby. The meeting went well enough; at least they could converse, and with Ricky putting the burden on Keith to talk about his life, Ricky didn't feel much pressure to make anything happen. Surprisingly, Keith was willing to talk about almost anything that first visit, almost as if he had been waiting for someone to enter his life, if only just to hear his thoughts and opinions. And when their time was over, Ricky once again courageously asked Keith if he would like to meet again. Keith said yes.

They set up another similar time and met not only once, but for a number of weeks. Eventually, Keith talked more and more about his artwork and photography and was obviously enjoying the attention of another person, even if he was older and not so cool. One interesting incident occurred, however: Ricky was looking at all of Keith's art supplies, noting that some of his brushes, marking pens, and art accessories were very nice. Keith replied with astonishing honesty, "Yes, well I pick those up for free from one of the local art stores. They don't know it though." Ricky immediately realized two things: 1) Keith was an amateur thief and a good one at that; 2) Keith had become quite open with him, more than Ricky thought he would be. Their relationship had certainly made some progress in openness. But what should he do? Ricky couldn't mince words. He told Keith that he had to either take the supplies back to the store or else go to the store and make restitution, confessing what he had done. Ricky was in for another surprise. Keith told him he was right and that he would make things right with the store. And that is exactly what he did. The store manager was surprised that any teenager would be so honest and forthcoming, so he told Keith that since Keith had both reimbursed him for the supplies and confessed, he was going to forgive him and forget it happened. Both Keith and Ricky grew up some during those weeks together but eventually Ricky had to move to another city and the relationship seemed to die out. Neither of them pursued it further but Ricky hoped that his courageous disciple investing enterprise had made a difference in a troubled teenage boy's life.

## Paul

Paul went to the state university in order to study, have a good time, party it up a little, and maybe find a serious girlfriend. Being raised Catholic meant very little to his collegiate aspirations, but he was somewhat conservative in both thinking and demeanor, so he wasn't going to let the party life ruin his academics. However, one day he was walking across campus heading back to his dorm when an older student came up to him and asked point blank, "Excuse me, but are you ready to die?" He was quite taken back by both the aggressiveness of the student and the assertiveness of such a heavy question. He answered "yes" but after the student walked away, he couldn't escape the nagging question. He wasn't sure he *was* ready to die. He decided to attend a meeting sponsored by a Christian group on the campus and in the coming weeks, he had the answer to the question that was disturbing him. He found Christ as his Lord and Savior, something that he had never been truly presented with in his upbringing. Eventually, he met another student from his hometown and that student told him that he attended RUF on campus. Paul said he wanted to go along with him and see what it was about. The RUF group was small but was also tight knit, something that was attractive to Paul. He liked being known, being a part of the group, and also loved the Bible teaching. He had never heard anything like it before.

Soon, the campus minister asked him if he wanted to get together. Paul was very pleased about that opportunity and jumped at it. First, it was just relationship building. But eventually, the relationship progressed to the point that Paul wanted the campus minister to challenge his thinking and answer all of the real questions that he had about the Bible and the Christian life. In time, Paul became a student leader in the group and had grown spiritually like a weed. As he moved into his senior year, he told the campus minister, "I really don't understand the big picture of the Bible. Is there anything I can read to help me see it?" The campus minister replied, "I can do better than that! I can meet with you one hour every week for the entire fall semester and we will do a walkthrough of the Bible, like a redemptive survey." Paul was elated. He was quite certain that he would never attend a Bible college or seminary, especially since his plans were to attend graduate school in physician's assistant training. But for fourteen weeks (or a full semester), he would be able to gain a Bible college level synopsis of the plan of redemption and hear material that was full of substance. Looking back, he stated to the campus minister, "I never knew I could learn so much in so little time and I'll always remember this material—it was so enlightening. Thank you!" Disciple investing can sometimes function like a college course or a semester-long relationship in which the disciple investing gets deep and the teaching pushes the learner. I'm not sure which is more exciting–seeing a new believer grow in understanding of all of the new and necessary concepts of Christian belief and behavior, or watching a seasoned believer go more deeply than he has ever gone before, preparing him for potential future leadership in the local church. What do you think?

## Aaron

Aaron grew up in a Christian home, attending a large, sound, Bible believing church and became a Christian at an early age. Very fit and athletic, he played a lot of sports and was very good. But when he went off to college, he tried out for the swim team as a walk-on but just missed the cut. He accepted it as the Lord's will but nonetheless, he was still discouraged. Not playing sports allowed him to get heavily involved with a ministry on campus and he was glad that he had a place to serve the Lord. He graduated and found a nice entry level job near the region of his hometown, but it seemed that he still struggled some with his discouragement. A Christian friend, Cal, noticed that Aaron wasn't completely himself, so he asked if they could get together. Aaron was glad to do so and they made plans to meet twice per month when possible. Cal made plans to walk Aaron through some topics about the Christian life using various Scripture passages. He was sure that the study of Scripture would be a great asset to Aaron. However, according to Cal, every time (or most every time, it seemed) they met, Aaron would turn the focus away from the Bible study topic and talk about all of his problems and struggles. Cal wondered if any of their time together was profitable. It seemed that all he was doing was listening and Aaron was making no progress at all. Eventually, Cal was transferred across the country and although the two of them would send each other Christmas greetings, their relationship subsided. They never spoke, only because their respective lives changed so much. Aaron got married and he and his wife started a family, while Cal and his wife had a number of children. Both were doing well in their jobs and were focused on their lives on separate coasts. One day about ten years later however, quite unexpectedly, Aaron called Cal to talk and to simply say, "Hello." The conversation was a great blessing as they shared about their expanded families, their jobs, their lives near two different US beaches and they reminisced about their time together many years earlier. Then, in an abrupt fashion, Aaron said, "Cal, there is something I want to tell you–actually I want to thank you." He continued, "All those times together, I know that I complained a lot and seemed really down. But I want you to know that a couple of years ago, I was diagnosed as clinically depressed. Since then, I have improved greatly and I am doing much better today. But, I had to call you, even though we haven't spoken in years, to let you know that for those couple of years where we were meeting regularly and you were just spinning your wheels with me, I believe that you saved my life. I'm not sure I would have continued living during that time unless you had supported me like you did. I feel like I owe some of my life to you. Again, thanks for being such a friend!" As they hung up, Cal was amazed at the role he had unknowingly played in Aaron's life. He thanked the Lord and felt a sense of blessing. Disciple investing doesn't always follow the agenda we try to set. Sometimes God uses us to see people through issues and perplexities that we don't even know are happening in their lives. Sometimes disciple investing is just being there or just being a listening ear and a supporter, a counselor for Christ's sake.

## Leon

Leon and Jeri grew up in Christian homes, both with two committed Christian parents. When they met each other after graduating from their respective colleges, it was love at first sight. Within the year, they were married and Leon became a traditional bread winner, with Jeri keeping the home and raising their two children. In time, Leon was transferred to a southern state which they would eventually call home. Leon's work was in human resources and he had gained quite the grasp of understanding what makes people tick and how to hire the right people for his corporation. He also had great business and financial acumen. The children grew up quickly and Leon and Jeri enjoyed the empty nest; so it seemed. They were in their early sixties now and the reality was that, because they had a little more extra time (although Leon was not retired yet), they quickly became other young couples' parents, in an *in loco parentis* or pseudo-parent function. On occasion, Leon had served as a deacon or elder in their various churches (they moved around the state a few times), but whether he was serving as a trained officer or not, Leon was always on the lookout for others' needs.

One day, Maria, a young Hispanic single mother of three, visited the church. It was obvious to everyone there that her life was in disarray. The children were young and quite unmanageable and there was no father to be seen. Church was not their natural habitat. But everyone accepted her and she felt so loved that she returned to the church the following week. Her reception was again very gracious, so she decided to attend regularly. Her children really liked the attention they received as well. In time, Leon and Jeri got to know Maria and as usual, they began serving her as surrogate parents, especially expressing love and affection to her three children. Maria worked two part time jobs, received some government assistance, lived in a modest apartment complex, and was trying to get by as she could. Leon decided that he and Jeri would make Maria and her children their special project. They invited her and the children to their home for meals together and they spent special time with her, listening to her problems and providing emotional support for her situation. They discovered that her husband left her right after the third child was born and the divorce was finalized just weeks prior to her visiting the church. Leon told Maria that they were going to meet together for at least five weeks and look at her finances, budget, spending, health benefits, and insurance. He was an expert in these matters. Jeri could contribute to any child raising guidance as needed but Leon would help her solve some of the family's financial pressures.

And that is what Leon did. He set out, through a few weekly meetings, to explain what biblical financial management should look like, including tithing of income and how God would take care of Maria and the children if she would learn and practice good stewardship of her money. Maria needed this common sense counsel, some of which she simply didn't know. She and her children's lives were changed through this sensible counsel, along with some adjustments and changes in expenditures. And Jeri's guidance about biblical discipline and respect for those in authority (in this case, one parent), plus her obvious love for the children, made quite the impression on the entire family as well. Maria and her family survived their ordeal. Leon and Jeri were conduits of the wisdom of Christ, wisdom that made them very effective disciple investors and transformed a frightened and insecure family into a home of much greater stability and hope. Disciple investing consists of taking the gifts and talents that God has given you and through Christ's Spirit, being used by him as he disciples his people, no matter where they are or what they are going through. What gift is in your hands?

## Questions for Reflection

1. Which case study do you relate to the most? Why?

2. Which case study taught you something new and how might you apply this newfound concept in your own life?

3. Which case study appears to be the most challenging to you personally? What makes it look so intimidating?

4. Considering the fact that each of these case studies are based on true stories, which case study surprised you the most? Why were you so surprised?

## Action Points

1. Begin to pray that God might place someone with a need for spiritual growth into your life.

2. List three personal motivations that would help you reach out to another person for the purpose of discipling him/her.

# 10

# An Excursion in Disciple Investing

THE FOLLOWING IS A fictional story but illustrates what a disciple investing relationship could look like. The description is realistic, however, and is based on my and others' efforts in the disciple investing adventure! Enjoy!

Trevor became a Christian as a teenager through the ministry of the neighborhood United Methodist Church youth group. Trevor had grown up in a more liberal-type denomination but had never heard the gospel, nor had he ever been confronted with the need to accept Jesus Christ as his personal Lord and Savior. Once he did accept Christ, he went to a lot of the meetings of the youth ministry. Eventually, he graduated from high school and went off to college, attending a major university. While there, he didn't attend church much but did help out with the local Young Life ministry. The college years were a time of some spiritual growth, but he spent more time doing outreach with high schoolers than anything else. Eventually, he received his bachelor's degree in business administration, found a job working with a large company that manufactures paper products, and moved to another city.

His life moved along rather well for a couple of years, but then he began wondering if he had any true meaning or purpose in his daily activities. He felt confident that he was a Christian, but he wasn't doing anything with Young Life. And although he had visited a couple of churches in town, he never found one that he liked or could settle into. His questions about purpose became his quest and he finally decided to find a church that he could call home. He visited a nice-sized church of about three hundred people that had a modest but attractive building. He went because a co-worker told him that they had a small singles and career group that was quite active. After a couple of visits, the assistant pastor, Joseph, who worked with the singles and career group, asked Trevor out for lunch. Lunch with Joseph was something Trevor really wanted to do because he used to have lunch meals with some of the Young Life staff while volunteering with them in college. He really enjoyed those lunchtime meals.

During the lunch, Joseph asked Trevor a little about his life, upbringing, family, experiences in college, and his situation at work. Trevor told him how he had become a Christian in high school and been involved in a church youth ministry, which led him to Young Life service while in college. But, Trevor told him, he really didn't know much at all about how to live the Christian life on a consistent basis. He always seemed to fail at his efforts. Joseph realized that what Trevor had done with the Young Life ministry while volunteering for them had not given him the depth he needed for actually walking with Christ. So, he asked Trevor if he might be interested in getting some input and help for growing more as a Christian. Trevor replied, "Would there really be someone who would help me in that way? I've actually prayed a few times that God would send me someone–anyone–to help show me the way. I've felt pretty guilty for the past two years or so." Joseph assured Trevor that someone would be willing to meet with him because the church had trained a handful of people in how to invest in the Christian growth of others who want to be serious disciples of Christ. He would have a young guy (only twenty eight years old) named Michael to contact him soon about getting together. As a matter of fact, if Trevor would be in church for worship on Sunday, Joseph would find Michael and introduce Trevor to him.

Sunday rolled around and Trevor headed to church with a sense that this could be a good day, especially if this "Michael guy" was going to be there. And indeed, after the service Joseph rushed over to Trevor to see him and then motioned over to Michael to come meet him. Michael seemed friendly enough, a little reserved but seemingly mature and genuinely interested in Trevor. He told Trevor that he would love to meet him for lunch sometime in the coming week and take him out to his favorite barbecue restaurant. And it would be his treat. Well, actually, it would be the church's treat because the elders had approved a budget item in which members could treat someone to lunch or dinner for the purpose of ministry, at least on the first get together.

Trevor was very happy about how all of this played out, and he and Michael decided to do a Saturday lunch before the big 2:00 p.m. basketball game that Trevor's alma mater was going to play that afternoon. When they met together for lunch, Trevor felt very comfortable. Michael was relaxed, had no real expectations, and was willing to listen to Trevor much like Joseph had during their lunch together. After they talked a little about different types of barbecue, the big game coming up, and what the weather was going to be like during the next week, the conversation got a little more personal and went something like this. . .

## First Meeting

*Michael:* "So Trevor, tell me about your family and your life growing up and all. . ."

*Trevor:* "I am one of three children, but we weren't very close. I was the youngest but the other two–a brother and a sister–were more than seven years older than me, so they lived in their world and I lived in mine. My mom and dad were mostly happy but I think I was kind of an "accident" or afterthought baby, so sometimes I felt like I was in the way. We went to church some, but it never meant much to me, or my parents really, so I lost interest until . . . until my friend Gary asked me to come to his youth group cookout at the Methodist Church. I liked that group and the kids there, so I kept going until one night a special speaker came to the meeting–he was a former NFL quarterback I think–and he challenged us to give our lives to Christ. I had never really heard it said that way before, but I knew that I needed to get right with God and to get my sins forgiven–I was pretty sneaky as a kid you know, although no one else really knew some of the things I had done. Anyhow, I gave my life to Christ and the speaker was right–I felt all clean and new, too! I didn't say much to my parents, but they were glad that I had found some friends and some good, clean activities with the Methodist Church, so they were happy to let me go there any time I wanted to. Those were some good days in my life."

*Michael:* "Well, what about in college?"

*Trevor:* "I guess that went pretty well. I wasn't too wild or anything but stayed up late on Saturday nights like everyone else and almost never went to church. But, it seemed okay because eventually, after the first semester–boy that was a rough one–I decided to volunteer for Young Life. I had heard of them while in high school but never went. I figured I could serve the Lord that way and not going to church would be okay. Don't you think so?"

*Michael* (knowing that it was too late now to tell him that he should have gotten involved in a local church while in college): "Well, I think it was good that you tried to do something for the Lord instead of just living like the usual hell-raising-type college student. That probably kept you from some things you might have regretted. And, by the way, what did you like best about working with Young Life?"

*Trevor:* "Oh, they really liked me; they were my friends and helped me to understand better how to accept those crazy high school students who came to the club meetings. They taught me some relational skills and helped me learn how to explain the gospel better for teenagers. Mostly though, I didn't grow a lot in my faith and I think I still need to understand the Bible better."

*Michael:* "So, what do you think you need to understand better about the Bible?"

*Trevor:* "I'm not sure I understand a lot of the basic doctrines, at least I'm not sure I could explain them if I was asked. I used to say the Apostle's Creed in the Methodist Church but I didn't fully understand all of the points. And I pray some–at least I try to pray–but I don't really know where to start."

*Michael:* "Well, if you are interested, I'd be glad to get together with you again and we can talk about some of those things–how about we get together and just talk about prayer? The Apostle's Creed can wait but maybe we can talk about that as well if there is time."

*Trevor:* "Wow, you would help me with stuff like that? Really, you don't have to."

*Michael:* "Oh, I'd love to do it and next meal will be my treat, not the church's. . . "

*Trevor:* "No, you can't do that! Not two times in a row."

*Michael:* "Listen, I'll get the next one and you get the one after that."

*Trevor:* "Okay."

*Michael:* "I'll be back in touch soon with a time and place."

*Trevor:* "Okay, see you then!"

*Michael:* "And hey–enjoy the big game; I hope your team pulls it off!"

*Trevor:* "Thanks!"

Michael checked his schedule and decided to take Trevor to Temple's Fried Chicken Hutt, which served the best fried chicken in town, and texted him to see if the time and place would work. It did, so they set their plans. Michael enjoyed this type of ministry–he would get to eat out at some of his favorite restaurants, while helping others in their walk with Christ. Prior to their second meeting, Michael checked with the church to see if they might have giveaway ESV Bibles kept in the church office for times like this, so he could take one for the next meeting with Trevor. They do, so he plans to pick it up on his way home from work on Monday.

## Next Meeting

Trevor and Michael met at Temple's Fried Chicken Hutt and found a quiet spot. Once their order came, Michael asked Trevor if he (Michael) could say a little blessing for the food (he didn't do that at the first meeting because he wanted to get to know Trevor a little better and not force the issue). That was fine with Trevor; he thought it was good to thank God in public even though he didn't do it very often himself. Michael kept the prayer short and simple and definitely avoided any heavy theological or pompous sounding terms because he thought that might be too showy and intimidating for Trevor.

As they began to eat, Michael talks to Trevor about last week's basketball game, the prospects for the next game, and whether or not his team will be highly ranked for the NCAA tournament. They discuss college basketball for about ten minutes and then the conversation went like this. . .

*Michael:* "So, did you have a good week last week? Anything new?"

*Trevor:* "Oh, it was about the usual. A lot of paper product orders for some reason, so I was really busy. I had a brief discussion with my boss about a possible promotion, but I'm waiting to see if something like that could really happen. I'm not going to get excited about it or anything. As they say, 'whatever happens, happens!'"

*Michael:* "Now there's something to pray about–I think the Lord would like to hear your feelings about that one!"

*Trevor:* "Really? I didn't think he gave much thought to stuff like that. I mean, there are huge wars, poverty, rampant diseases being spread, people that need to be saved–come on! He's not thinking about my job opportunities is he?"

*Michael:* "Oh yes, he knows the number of hairs on your head and his eye is on the sparrow. He cares about all of his creatures and their needs!"

*Trevor:* "Well, I guess I could pray about that. I do pray some most every day. Sometimes, it's just when I'm driving to work or I fire up a fast one when I'm in a sticky spot. I guess I could add a job to my–ha ha–my prayer list. It's not much of a list."

*Michael:* "Okay, I say let's look at the subject of prayer for the next thirty minutes and talk about it. What do you think?"

*Trevor:* "Sounds good to me."

*Michael:* "Let's look at a familiar passage about prayer in the Bible and see what it says. I brought my Bible and either you can look it up on your iPhone or you can use this Bible that I would like to give you–it's a recent translation called the English Standard Version or the ESV and it's a really good translation."

*Trevor:* "Uh, I was going to use my iPhone but I would love to have the Bible. I'd like to have the book form in my hands; I still read lots of hardbound type books in addition to Kindle books. Thanks!"

*Michael:* "It's not an expensive edition but if you like it, eventually you can buy a leather one that is a little more attractive and will hold up better."

*Trevor:* "This is great!"

*Michael:* "Okay, let's open to Matthew 6, which is the Lord's prayer–I bet you've prayed that a few times before!"

*Trevor:* "Yes I have and I think I could recite it by memory."

*Michael:* "Well, I won't ask you to do that, but I guess if we both started reciting it out loud here in the restaurant, some other people might bow their heads and join in, ha ha!"

*Trevor:* "Yes, that's funny–we won't try that."

*Michael:* "Let's look at Matthew 6:9–13. There's other stuff about prayer in the first few verses, but let's just look at the Lord's Prayer. Take a couple of minutes to read it and maybe think about it a little as you read. Take your time. Let me know when you're done."

Trevor read the passage silently–it only took about one minute–and even while he did so, Michael silently prayed that God would use this discussion for his glory and honor and to help Trevor, as well as Michael himself to grow.

> 9 *Pray then like this: "Our Father in heaven, hallowed be your name.* 10 *Your kingdom come, your will be done, on earth as it is in heaven.* 11 *Give us this day our daily bread,* 12 *and forgive us our debts, as we also have forgiven our debtors.* 13 *And lead us not into temptation, but deliver us from evil."*

*Trevor:* "Alright, I'm done."

*Michael:* "Great; let's ask some questions and also consider the passage. First off, how do we usually *begin* our personal prayers? What usually are our prayers' main subject matter?"

*Trevor:* "I'm not sure what you mean, but I think most of my prayers are about me."

*Michael:* "Yes, that's what I meant. It is easy to pray for ourselves and make a lot of personal requests to him, kind of like a Christmas present list. But how does the Lord's Prayer start?"

*Trevor:* "Oh, I see; it starts with God, not us!"

*Michael:* "Yes! And how is God addressed?"

*Trevor:* "Our Father in heaven, hallowed be your name. Hey–it doesn't say 'who *art*' and '*thy* name' in this version. That's different from the way we did it in the Methodist church. But I guess it doesn't matter."

*Michael:* "No, that's not too important. But let me ask, 'Why *is* God addressed this way?'"

*Trevor:* "As Father? I'm sure it is because he loves us and takes care of us like a good father would. I know some people don't have good fathers but God is good, and a good father would look out for his children."

*Michael:* "Yes, we have a special relationship with God as his children, if we have repented of our sins and trusted Christ as our Savior. As a matter of fact, John 1:12 says, 'But to all who did receive him, who believed in his name, he gave the right to become children of God. . .' So, it is rather unbelievable that God considers us as his children. He adopts us, really."

*Trevor:* "Yes and I do believe I am his child. When I asked Christ into my life in high school, I became a new person and felt like I was God's child. I was really changed. I guess that means that he really will hear my prayer. He's not just some big being in outer space that wouldn't care about people. Boy, I like that idea!"

*Michael:* "Yes, that is right–that is why we need to pray about that possible job promotion and your peace about it."

*Trevor:* "Yeah. . . "

*Michael:* "So, why the clause 'in heaven?'"

*Trevor:* "Well, that's what I was just saying. He is in heaven, so he is a great being, but he is also a father, like someone nearby. He's close. That's so great to think about."

*Michael:* "What else does this first section say?"

*Trevor:* "It says, 'hallowed be your name'. That is a strange phrase but I know it means something about how special his name is, right?"

*Michael:* "Yes, it means his name is holy and we ought to be reverent with it. We should never misuse his name."

*Trevor:* "Uh oh. And I think that is one of the Ten Commandments too isn't it? I really mess up there sometimes."

*Michael:* "Yes, I've read that Americans say this is the hardest commandment to keep. Do you think so?"

*Trevor:* "Yes, I think so, but I don't remember all of the others."

Michael: "We can talk about that another time."

*Trevor:* "Let's do. I need to brush up on the Ten Commandments. They're like early in the Old Testament somewhere right?"

*Michael:* "Yes, that's right. But let me ask you this: What does a name represent?"

*Trevor:* "Well, I guess a name represents the person. People know you by your name and you respond to it."

*Michael:* "Yes, it speaks about who we are and also, about our character. We honor others when we properly use their name. How do Christians give *honor* to God's name?"

*Trevor:* "I guess by not swearing by it and using it flippantly. I guess by being thoughtful whenever you say God's name. I know I could do better and it would probably mean more when I pray to God if I haven't used his name without thinking about who he really is the rest of the time. Wow, this is really helpful. When I pray, I know that God will treat me like a good father, but he is also very great and must be treated with great respect–like you said, 'holy.' That really helps. I think I'll put this in practice before I go to bed tonight."

*Michael:* "That sounds great Trevor. And we've spent a lot of time discussing this. And there's a lot more of the Lord's Prayer to consider. Would you like to get together again sometime soon? Really, I can do this for a few weeks if you like or maybe even longer, but that's up to you."

*Trevor:* "Well, if you're willing, I'm willing. Let's try again in the next couple of weeks."

Michael: "How about before your college team's basketball game next Tuesday night? No dinner, just come to my place and I'll have some refreshments. We'll talk for an hour or so and then, tipoff!"

Trevor: "Perfect, except you come to my place and I'll take care of the party items and we'll watch the game on my big screen TV! Game?"

Michael: "Yes, game on! I'll see you then."

Trevor: "Great! And thanks again for the fried chicken. Temple's is a lot better than Church's any day!"

Michael: "See ya!"

Trevor: "Yes, later."

## Next Meetings

In the ensuing meetings, Michael could continue the discussion on the Lord's Prayer. Here are some sample questions he could use (with some possible answers in italics):

Verse 9 (continued): *Pray then like this: "Our Father in heaven, hallowed be your name."*

1. When we think of honoring God's name, we can do so by praising his name. How much of prayer should be praise, thanks and asking?

2. What is the difference between praise *(acknowledging God's character)* and thanks *(acknowledging God's blessings)*?

3. What types of things can we thank God for?

4. Name all the attributes of God for which we can praise him:

5. What might *praise* do for the heart of the Christian? What does it demonstrate about the heart of the believer? *(He has joy in God himself)*

6. What might *thanks* do for the heart of the Christian? What does it demonstrate about the heart of the believer? *(He is humbled and dependent)*

Verse 10: *"Your kingdom come, your will be done, on earth as it is in heaven."*

1. How does a Christian learn God's will? (*His word (#1); gifts and abilities; circumstances; counsel of others who are godly; prayer; taking steps of faith*)

2. What is God's number one goal (i.e., his will) for the Christian? (*Christ's Lordship; to live for his glory*)

3. What does it mean for God's kingdom to come? What are we looking for?

4. How great will God's kingdom be on the earth? Any idea? Will it be worldwide? How do you know if God's kingdom is established in your heart? In your city?

Verse 11: *"Give us this day our daily bread,"*

1. How do you make this prayer for "basic survival" relevant in the twentieth century? What word/words would a twenty-first century person insert/substitute instead of *daily bread*, i.e., "give us this day our_____"?

2. How are we *dependent* upon God?

3. Is it okay to have more than the necessities of life–to have luxuries? Why would someone pray for luxuries?

Verse 12: (see also verses 14–15) *"and forgive us our debts, as we also have forgiven our debtors."*

1. If Christians are forgiven, why do they have to *ask* God for forgiveness? (*Discuss absolute, final forgiveness vs. daily, relational forgiveness*)

2. What are "our debts"? (*Sins–anything we do against God for which we must pay sin's penalty*) Why do you think some churches use the word "trespasses" instead of "debts"?

3. Why is our forgiveness from God contingent on our forgiving others? (*See Matthew 6:14–15 and Matthew 18:23–35*)

Verse 13: *"And lead us not into temptation, but deliver us from evil."*

1. What are some of our daily temptations? Are they any different for men and women? If so, how?

2. Does God ever *lead us* into temptation? Cf. *James 1:13–14*

3. What is the difference between *temptation* and *God's testing* (trials)?

4. When tempted to sin (e.g., lust, lying at work or on your taxes, gossip, etc.), how do we escape, i.e., how are we delivered from evil (Satan)? How does this play out, i.e., what do we *think/do* as Christians to find this deliverance?

## Continued Meetings and a Deepened Relationship/ Friendship

Trevor and Michael continued to meet. As a matter of fact, they met regularly for two years. Eventually, Trevor's promotion led to a transfer out of the town and after he moved, the two of them stayed in touch by phone and through other means provided by the wonder of modern technology. During those two years together, they talked about the Ten Commandments, the Lordship of Christ, how to win over temptation, anxiety, and worry, God's sovereignty, suffering and joy, and a few other topics. All they did to facilitate their meetings was to open the Bible to a passage on the topic and ask questions about it, while sharing what each other understood were God's answers. Sometimes Trevor had actually learned some truths that Michael didn't already know, which was a pleasant surprise for both of them. As a matter of fact, a few times, they had one or two other guys show up to join them which made the discussions even more interesting and stimulating. And the last three remaining months of Trevor's time in town, he met with two students from the local community college and did the same type of discussions with them by himself. Disciple investing had become a way of life for Trevor just as it was for Michael, and Trevor was certain that he could always find someone who would be willing to meet with him. He was now on the lookout for people in his new church, on the job, in his neighborhood, and in his sports clubs.

## Questions for Reflection

1. What do you think went well during the first meeting between Trevor and Michael? What might you have done differently?

2. What do you think about the way Michael led the next meeting that the two of them had together? Did he handle the passage on the Lord's Prayer in a helpful manner?

3. Could you think of another passage on prayer that Michael could have used to help Trevor? If so, why would you choose that passage and what would you emphasize?

4. What are some other topics that you might address or questions you might raise about Trevor's present situation and why?

## Action Points

1. Contact your pastor (or a leader in your church) or a person in a local parachurch ministry (college or youth ministry) and ask them if they have the name of a person (or persons) with whom you could meet to explore a disciple investing relationship.

2. For the next two weeks, choose a convenient time and set aside a few minutes of the day to pray to the Lord of the harvest that he will send a person with whom you can disciple invest.

# Conclusion

WE HAVE SPENT OUR time looking at the nature, the qualifications, and the cost of disciple investing. Being a disciple is following and learning from Jesus and also learning to love Jesus, the living Lord and Savior. Becoming a disciple is a process which involves a full-orbed, multi-dimensional impact by the Holy Spirit in the life of the follower of Jesus Christ. Discipleship is simply God changing us to be more and more like his Son. Disciple investing means that a follower of Jesus can serve Jesus by helping others know him better and become like him. Jesus is the great Discipler of all of his followers, those whom he has called to "come after him." But, he uses us as we invest in the spiritual well-being of others. Disciple investing fulfills both the Great Commandment and the Great Commission. We love God, we love others, and we love both God and others by making disciples of all nations, baptizing them in the name of the Father, and of the Son, and of the Holy Spirit; teaching them to observe all that Christ has commanded us.

We also discovered that we must meet certain qualifications in order to be capable disciple investors. Those would include a vibrant walk with Christ, in which he is alive to us personally, the ability to be a friend to others, demonstrating a faith that God is at work and will use us in the lives of others, as well as fighting sin so that purity of life is a goal. Further, we should live the Christian life by abiding in Christ as a flowing fountain in our lives while exhibiting consistency in our Christian walk, (as opposed to hypocrisy). A disciple investor should also see the Bible as his foundation for everything he does and should be continually growing in his biblical understanding, with a willingness to be taught and to learn.

Certain attitudes are necessary in order to carry forth disciple investing in a fruitful manner. First and foremost, we must be gospel driven. Living out an understanding of God's grace in our lives is what is meant by being gospel driven. Having received grace from the Lord for our own

127

sins and failures leads us to act in grace toward the disciple. It can be no other way. Like the Apostle Paul, we must live a life of love for the other person, a love that includes passion and compassion for him. And a great complement to love is the spirit of humility, an attitude that we, as disciple investors, are learning from Jesus and can also learn from the disciple. We don't lord ourselves over the other. Knowing that becoming like Christ is a process (sanctification) and takes time, translates into the fruit of patience. And although we may perceive that our role is one of constant input and teaching, the effective disciple investor understands that a listening ear is possibly the most valuable tool she has with which to help the disciple. Lastly, spiritual parenting, nurturing others like a mother and exhorting them like a father, is a key source of motivation and an attitude that spawns selflessness on behalf of the disciple.

Further, disciple investing is costly. Pouring ourselves into another person or other persons requires being equipped to do the job, particularly in knowing the Scriptures. It also involves making time and expending the necessary energy to "work" for the sake of the other person. Attention is essential to maintaining the relationship and we must enact follow up in order to assess how the person is doing, especially if he is struggling or lacking in responsiveness regarding overtures to meet together.

The Five "I's" also demonstrate the cost of disciple investing: 1) Interest–genuine concern for the spiritual success and well-being of another person; 2) Ideas–creating ways to actually meet people who need help; 3) Intention–making plans to get started; 4) Implementation–actually doing something concrete, enacting the plan; and 5) Involvement–recognizing that now you will be committed to seeing the other person through the good and the bad, the positives and the trials. There normally is no turning back at this stage.

We briefly looked together at both Jesus's method of selecting and associating with men whom he believed had potential. In doing so, we realized that one person can indeed make a difference. You can be that person. And observing Paul's approach, we learned that he became very engaged personally with his disciples, communicating with them, giving time, attention and focus to them, while also sacrificing himself for them. Furthermore, he set a personal example for them, praised their progress, and prayed for them. Amazingly, he recognized that those in whom he was investing could mutually contribute to his comfort, joy, and encouragement. His disciples could contribute to his well-being, even as he contributed to theirs. He also radiated a positive attitude in trials, one that came from being united with Christ. And ultimately, his ministry emanated gifts of preaching and teaching, using the Word of God as the powerful tool that it was, in the lives of his disciples. Finally, we saw that organic disciple investing, i.e., recognizing that the body of Christ and the community of believers, (along with the means of grace) contributes to and complements the disciple investor's efforts, and takes the pressure off of the disciple investor. We saw that we have help from others in our efforts to aid the disciple's spiritual progress.

In chapter 5, we provided a long, but non-exhaustive, list of character qualities in the life of a true and growing disciple. We can observe progress and fruit, and although outward behavior may be misleading, there are a number of attributes that exemplify the life of a growing and maturing disciple. In some ways, these attributes can be measured, not mechanically, but in the sense that, as people look at their own hearts, lives, passions and practices, they can explain or express their progress in or desires toward becoming Christ-like.

In chapter 6, we noted that there are always problems working with other people. As with ourselves, others have generic people problems and we must deal with and patiently address them. The disciple very possibly might express resistance in the process or in the development of the relationship, causing much frustration. She may also be inconsistent in her behavior, or simply lack commitment to the relationship or the expectations or activities needed to sustain it. Hopeful but failed agendas may further discourage us as disciple investors, although God often uses them serendipitously in the life of the disciple, working through us in ways that we cannot see at the time.

Diagnosis and counseling, as covered in a lengthy chapter 7, is one of the most important aspects of disciple investing. We noted that there are, by profession, all sorts of "Christians" and thus we need to discover what a person means when he defines himself as a Christian. The ministry of asking questions is absolutely crucial to the task of the disciple investor. We must ask questions of the individual, in order to understand him, as well as of the Scriptures, in order for the individual to understand them. Ultimately, the disciple investor wants to meet the need of the individual with a helpful answer from the Word of God. Scripture is the answer for true soul searching. Chapter 8 supplied a long list of areas of need that could exist in the life of any disciple, as well as appropriate Scriptures that could speak to the need of the hearer. The Word of God does have the answers for the needs of our hearts!

Chapter 9 provided a number of actual, although adapted, cases of real disciple investing situations, lending themselves as a guide to the aspiring disciple investor. These sample cases should also serve as an inspiration, helping us to realize that disciple investing, by broad definition, is used by God to impact others' lives. Disciple investing has the potential to be transformative in both the disciple investor's life and the life of the person in whom she is investing.

Finally, chapter 10 provided an imaginary but helpful example of a disciple investing conversation that was occurring in a growing relationship. Although not an actual situation, it reflects what the author has seen during the accumulation of his and others' disciple investing efforts and provides a model of how a one-to-one disciple relationship could be initiated and consequently transpire. The hope of this chapter is that it will furnish a realistic walk-through of a disciple investing possibility and contribute to the inspiration of those who might hesitate to jump into the disciple investing responsibility.

Ultimately, this book is written to help that reader understand that disciple investing is possible and you can do it! You'll never regret trying as you trust in the Lord! Do you hear Jesus calling? I hope that you do!

# Appendix
## Measuring The Progress Of A Growing Believer

### CHRISTIAN WALK ASSESSMENT

#### Measuring Progress Survey

How do we evaluate one's becoming more like Christ?
(CHOOSE THE ANSWER ON EACH QUESTION THAT BEST
DESCRIBES YOU)

PLEASE ANSWER THE QUESTIONS TO
THE BEST OF YOUR ABILITY

BACKGROUND

1.  I have been a Christian:

    a.  All my life–I have never known a time without Christ in my life

    b.  In young childhood–before age seven

    c.  In grade school

    d.  During middle school

    e.  During high school

    f.  In college

    g.  Later in life (after college age)

    h.  Very recently–I am a new Christian

2. I grew up . . .

    a. In a non-Christian home–neither parent was a Christian

    b. In an atheistic home with no sympathies for or inclinations toward Christianity whatsoever

    c. In a Christian home–both parents were committed, practicing Christians

    d. In a Christian home but neither parent was overly committed to Christ or his church

    e. In a partially Christian home–one of my parents was a committed Christian

    f. In a religious home, but it was not the Christian religion

    g. Other: _____

## PERSONAL DISCIPLINES AND SPIRITUAL NOURISHMENT

3. I try to set aside a time *every* day to pray:    Yes    No

4. I read my Bible . . .

    a. Every day–top priority

    b. Most every day

    c. Three times per week

    d. When I am able

    e. Very rarely

5. My *relationship with the Bible* could best be described as . . .

    a. Hearing it read or preached

    b. Reading it personally

    c. Reading it but also attending Bible studies in order to learn more

    d. Reading it but also studying it personally

    e. Reading it, studying it some, and also memorizing Bible verses

    f. All of the above, as well as setting aside time to meditate on the Bible for life change and application

6. In regard to *reading the Bible* . . .

  a. I have read through the entire Bible once or more in my life

  b. I have read through the entire New Testament but not much of the Old Testament

  c. I have read a lot of the New Testament and a lot of the Old Testament

  d. I have only read portions of the New Testament

  e. I haven't read much of the Bible at all

7. I have structured *personal devotions* (intentional, private prayer and Bible reading, i.e., a Quiet Time):

  a. Every day–morning *and* evening

  b. Every day–morning *or* evening

  c. Almost every day

  d. Every other day

  e. On occasion

  f. I rarely have a personal Quiet Time with God

8. When I have *personal devotions* (a Quiet Time), I spend this much time with God:

  a. Five minutes/day

  b. Seven to ten minutes/day

  c. Fifteen minutes/day

  d. Thirty minutes/day

  e. More than thirty minutes/day

  f. I really don't keep track of the time

9. My personal devotions would be described as:

  a. Just starting: I read devotional material and guides and pray their prayers

  b. Just starting with the habit of some Bible reading and personal prayers

  c. I read both devotional booklets/guides and the Bible and pray in response to both

d. I read the Bible only (alone) in a committed manner and pray based on what I read

e. I read the Bible most every day and try to think about what I have read during the day

f. I read the Bible most every day and sometimes study what I am reading; I also pray

g. I set aside time to read the Bible devotionally and pray twice per day (usually morning and evening)

h. I set aside time to read the Bible devotionally and also study the Bible during my devotional times, sometimes using study helps or a commentary

10. My *prayer life* could best be described as . . .

a. Praying for myself

b. Praying for myself with some thanksgiving

c. Praying for myself, including lots of confession of sin and repentance

d. Praying for myself, confession, thanksgiving, and lots of praise to the Lord (ACTS)

e. Praying for myself but praying a lot for others (intercession)

f. Praying through the elements of "The Lord's Prayer"

g. Praying privately only

h. Praying privately but also praying with others in a group (corporate setting)

i. Prayer as a regular conversation with God

j. Leading others in prayer and to practice praying regularly

k. Setting aside long blocks of time (an hour or more) on a regular basis to pray

l. Praying seriously, with an element of fasting included

11. In regard to *memorizing the Bible* . . .

a. I have memorized Bible verses since I was a small child

b. I have memorized a few Bible verses over the years

    c. I have gone through a Bible verse memory program and have memorized a lot of verses

    d. I have tried to memorize Bible verses but can never remember or retain the verses

    e. I have never really tried to memorize any Bible verses

    f. I think that the memorization of Bible verses is overrated

    g. I don't really see the relevance of memorizing Bible verses

12. Besides the Bible, my *favorite Christian book(s)* I have read is (are):

    a.

    b.

    c.

    d.

## PERSONAL GROWTH

13. In regard to my *relationship to personal sin* . . .

    a. I am aware of certain sins in my life and feel bad about them

    b. I am aware of certain sins in my life and repent of them

    c. I am aware that my heart is filled with sinfulness and I constantly need forgiveness

    d. I am constantly aware of my sins and sinfulness, but rejoice constantly in God's certain forgiveness and grace

    e. I am often dealing with specific sins in my life, especially those with which I struggle, and I confess them with hatred, claiming God's forgiveness

    f. I am well aware that my sins come from deep heart issues, and I live with a conscious awareness of both my sinfulness and the needs of my heart to deal with my sins

    g. I am constantly fighting my sins and understand that the Christian life involves spiritual warfare, a constant battle with my sin and the enemy, the devil

h. I am constantly fighting my sins and understand that the Christian life involves mortification, i.e., I must constantly kill the sinful desires and deeds of my fallen heart

i. I am constantly fighting my sins and have asked another believer to help me be accountable for my patterns of sinful behavior or the sins that seem to plague me

j. I am constantly aware of my sins and view the normal Christian life as one of daily, if not moment-by-moment, confession and repentance of my personal sins

14. As related to *understanding God's love* . . .

a. I am not certain that God loves me at all

b. I often think that God loves me conditionally, based mostly upon my behavior or failures and successes in the Christian life

c. I am not certain that God loves me all the time

d. I know God loves me because I can feel his love in my life

e. I believe God loves me and usually I feel loved by God

f. I am secure in God's love and know that his love will never leave me

g. I experience God's love every day and a life based on God's love is a way of life for me

15. As related to understanding Christian love . . .

a. I find it very difficult to love others at all, either with my own love or the love of God

b. I am struggling to love others but am learning how to do so

c. I envy others who know God loves them and who can love others based on that love

d. I am learning to put others first and love them in that way

e. I understand that "agape" love means that God sacrificed his Son for me and that I should love others sacrificially

f. I am learning or have learned to love my enemies and to pray for those who persecute me

g. I would willingly give my own life for the sake of another or others out of love for God

16. As far as growing in conquering my personal pride and *learning humility* ...

   a. I am still filled with overwhelming personal pride and it hinders me in relationships with others

   b. Although not filled with pride, it is still a very present struggle in my Christian life

   c. I am truly learning what it means to say "Jesus is Lord" in my own life

   d. I am very aware of my "old life" without Christ and that alone humbles me at least some

   e. I know that personal pride is both offensive as well as destructive in my own life and my relationships with others, and is an issue with which I must deal

   f. God is breaking me and I am slowly learning the beauty of the path of lowliness, humility, and service

   g. I think that I am actually learning what it means to "consider others better than myself"

17. As for growing in *theological understanding of Scripture* ...

   a. I'm not sure what the word or concept "theological" means or is expressing

   b. I understand the four basic points of a gospel presentation but am not certain that I could explain them

   c. I can explain some of the gospel categories but want to know much more than the basics

   d. I understand that there are a number of theological categories and I would like to study all of them enough to know the difference

   e. I understand what systematic theology means and want to learn more so that I can find biblical answers to my and others' questions

   f. I have read some theological books, such as A.W. Tozer's Knowledge of the Holy and J.I. Packer's Knowing God (or something similar)

g. I have read portions of what is known as a systematic theology book

h. I could probably teach a class in basic systematic theology

MINISTRY AND CHURCH

18. In *the past*, I have been involved in . . .

a. A church ministry of some sort
(What type: _____)

b. A campus ministry
(Which one: _____)

c. A camp ministry
(Which one: _____)

d. A parachurch ministry
(Which one: _____)

e. Other ministry
(Which one: _____)

f. I have no past ministry experience

19. My relationship with a *local church* is:

a. I don't attend a local church

b. I am not a member of a church and don't have a church to join

c. I am not a member of a church although I do attend local churches sometimes

d. I am not a member of a church but am considering joining a church

e. I am a member of the church I grew up in

f. I am a member of the last church I attended

g. I am a member of a church I once attended but no longer attend

h. I am a member of a church and both attend and participate in that church

i. I have membership in more than one church

20. As for *present ministry*:

    a. I am presently not doing any type of ministry

    b. I am not doing anything officially but try to minister when and where I can

    c. I serve unofficially in a local church

    d. I assist others in a ministry in a local church

    e. I am pursuing an internship with a local church or other ministry

    f. I am presently an intern with a local church

    g. I am on staff (part-time) with a local church

    h. I am on staff (full-time) with a local church

    i. I am an ordained minister but not presently serving a local church

    j. I am an ordained minister and presently serving a church

21. In regard to my *personal finances and giving . . .*

    a. I give a little something on occasion to ministries that appeal to me

    b. I give a little something on occasion to the local church of my choice

    c. I give a little something *regularly* to the local church of my choice

    d. I give a significant amount regularly to my own local church but don't presently tithe

    e. I give a tithe (10 percent) of my income to my own local church and other worthy ministries

    f. I give a tithe (10 percent) of my income to my own local church, and in addition to the tithe, I give above the tithe to other ministries (grace giving or faith promise giving)

    g. I give well above the tithe of my income to my local church and also give sacrificially (above the tithe so that it hurts) to both my church and other worthy ministries

22. As far as learning to be *a servant . . .*

    a. I am aware that service should be a part of the Christian life

b. I watch others serve and wonder how I could serve

c. I realize both the joys and personal benefits of serving others and want to do more

d. When others are recruiting someone for service, I am interested in helping serve

e. I volunteer for simple tasks without being asked

f. I volunteer for bigger jobs without being asked as long as I am able to do the task

g. I serve by leading and involving others in service projects

h. I organize and lead service projects and opportunities

23. In relation to the attribute of *Christian sacrifice* . . .

a. I still seem to sacrifice others for my own needs

b. I only make sacrifices when others demand them of me or guilt me into them

c. I understand something of the great sacrifice that Christ made for my salvation and know that I need to grow in sacrificial living

d. The words "sacrifice" and "suffering" have become a part of my Christian vocabulary in a positive way and I wish to practice a self-sacrificing lifestyle

e. I am aware of Jesus's call to take up my cross and deny myself if I wish to follow him, and I consider this call to be an important part of my Christian life

f. I consciously make daily self-sacrifices because I am motivated to be more Christ-like

g. I actively pursue opportunities of service that require sacrifices on my part and rejoice to do so

24. When describing my progress in the area of *spiritual warfare* . . .

a. I do not really know what this means or what it involves personally

b. I have come to realize that the Christian life is not easy and being a Christian does not mean that all I will ever experience is a constant spiritual high

    c. It certainly seems like a reality that I am aware of in my own Christian life but I don't think I am progressing in my struggle

    d. I am learning to fight sin and Satan as a daily reality in the Christian life

    e. I am striving more and more to use both the "means of grace" and spiritual disciplines in order to overcome in the struggle of spiritual warfare

    f. I am vigorously fighting sin and Satan, and sense that I am experiencing some victory over nagging sin(s) in my life

## OUTREACH

25. I spend *time with non-Christians*:

    a. Every day

    b. Every other day, it seems

    c. Regularly

    d. Weekly

    e. Off and on, depending on the demands of my schedule

    f. I just don't run into non-Christians

    g. Rarely

    h. Never and I would like to improve

    i. Never and I need a lot more motivation to do so

26. As far as *evangelism* (sharing my faith) goes . . .

    a. I've never had much interest in doing evangelism

    b. I have made my profession of faith in Christ public and want others to know

    c. I know outreach is a responsibility, but I don't really know what to do about it

    d. I am concerned for the lost and unchurched and want to help them

    e. I get excited about evangelism and want to find out more about how to do it

    f. I take the initiative and try to do it, although feebly

g. I'm zealous for evangelism and do it when I can

h. I have been trained and try to evangelize to others when the opportunity presents itself

27. The last time I was able to *tell someone about Christ* and their need for Christ was:

a. Recently, in the last week or so

b. Recently, in the last month or so

c. It's been a few months

d. It's been over one year

e. I've never really spoken to another person explicitly about their relationship to Christ

f. I've never been trained in evangelism and explaining the gospel

g. The thought of personal evangelism frightens me because I have never been trained

28. As far as *understanding the gospel* . . .

a. I point others to places or people who can explain the gospel

b. I can tell others how I became a Christian

c. I can explain my "personal testimony" of faith in Christ in a way that is organized, makes sense, and is gospel-centered

d. I have gospel literature (pamphlets or tracts) that I can give to someone who wants to know the gospel

e. I can explain a simple, four point presentation of the gospel

f. I have been trained in clearly presenting the gospel through an organized program

g. I could walk through the New Testament with someone else and point out the verses that would present the gospel

h. I could walk through the *Old* Testament with someone else and point out the verses that would present the gospel

i. I have a gospel outline and many Bible verses memorized and could present the gospel at will most any moment that the need presents itself

j.  I am trained in Christian apologetics and can carry on both debates and philosophical conversations about my faith

# Bibliography

Bonhoeffer, Dietrich. *Life Together*. Harper and Row, Inc. 1954. Print.

Coleman, Robert. *The Master Plan of Evangelism*. Grand Rapids: F.H. Revell, 1963. Print.

Grubb, Norman, *C.T. Studd*. Fort Washington: Christian Literature Crusade, 1972. Print.

Guiness, Os. *Doubt*. InterVarsity Christian Fellowship/Lion Corporation, 1976. Print.

Lee, Helen. "5 Kinds of Christians." *Leadership Journal*. October 1, 2007. Print.